MCQs
and extended matching
questions for the MRCS

W E G Thomas MS FRCS

Consultant Surgeon and
Clinical Director of Surgery
Royal Hallamshire Hospital, Sheffield, UK

**The
Medicine**

**Publishing
Company**

First published 2002

ISBN 0-9532598-3-8

A catalogue record for this title is available from the British Library.

The Medicine Publishing Company Limited
62 Stert Street
Abingdon
Oxfordshire
OX14 3UQ
UK

Tel: +44(0)1235 542800
Fax: +44(0)1235 554692
e-mail: admin@medicinepublishing.co.uk

For further information on The Medicine Publishing Company visit
www.medicinepublishing.co.uk

Typeset, printed and bound by Emirates Printing Press, Dubai.

Preface

The MRCS examination currently includes two major papers of
Multiple Choice Questions and Extended Matching Questions
covering basic sciences and systematic clinical topics. In preparation
for this part of the examination there is no substitute for good on-the
spot clinical training on a surgical rotation, supplemented by a
formal teaching programme such as the distance learning STEP
Course. However astute candidates will also prepare themselves for
the examination by practicing their examination technique. Such
preparation for the papers includes repeated practice at answering
Multiple Choice Questions and particularly the Extended Matching
Questions that may not be so familiar to some candidates. It is
invaluable to have experience in handling such questions before
being faced by them in the examination. Such practice not only
familiarises the candidate with the format of the questions they are
likely to encounter in the examination, but also helps consolidate
their knowledge.

The questions in this book have been modelled on the format used in
the MRCS examination and have been grouped as to subject matter
according to the configuration of Core or System modules as laid out
in the MRCS syllabus. The questions have been based on
authoritative articles published in *SURGERY* that were specifically
written with the MRCS candidate in mind. It is hoped that by
working their way through these questions, the potential MRCS
candidate will not only become better informed and surgically more
knowledgeable, but will also be better equipped to face the rigours
of the two MCQ papers.

W E G Thomas
Sheffield 2001

Contents

Core Modules

System Modules

MCQs

1 Day Case Anaesthesia

Which of the following statements are true?

A ☐ Patients with a BMI > 34 should be excluded from day surgery

B ☐ Patients with severe systemic disease and some functional limitation are graded as ASA 4

C ☐ Non-steroidal anti-inflammatory drugs should not be used in day case surgery

D ☐ Before day case surgery, patients may drink clear fluids up to about 3 hours preoperatively

E ☐ Spinal anaesthesia is contraindicated in the day case setting

2 Principles of Anaesthesia

With regard to anaesthesia:

A ☐ Intravenous ketamine decreases myocardial contractility

B ☐ Cardiac depression caused by local anaesthetic agents should be treated with intravenous atropine

C ☐ Surgery with a general anaesthetic should be cancelled if the patient has allergic or vasomotor rhinitis

D ☐ All intravenous anaesthetic agents are lipid soluble

E ☐ Intramuscular analgesia does not satisfactorily control pain

3 Prevention of Nerve Injuries in the Anaesthetized Patient

In patients in whom there is nerve damage during anaesthesia:

A ☐ Axonotmesis means failure of nerve conduction due to loss of myelin

B ☐ Complete recovery is unusual

C ☐ Women are five times more vulnerable to ulnar nerve damage than men

D ☐ The radial nerve may be injured when a tourniquet is applied

E ☐ The buccal branch of the facial nerve may be endangered by a tight-fitting facemask

MCQs

1 Day Case Anaesthesia

A True

B ASA grade 4 patients are those with severe systemic disease which is incapacitating and a constant threat to life. Patients with severe systemic disease and *some* functional limitation are graded as ASA 3.

C There is no bar to the use of non-steroidal anti-inflammatory agents (e.g. diclofenac, ibuprofen) in day case surgery using either the rectal or oral route. The use of some NSAIDs is controversial because of their effect on haemostasis but there is little conclusive evidence that their use increases perioperative bleeding.

D True

E Developments in the design of spinal needles means that spinal anaesthesia is no longer contraindicated in the day case setting and may have advantages over general anaesthesia.

2 Principles of Anaesthesia

A Unlike other intravenous anaesthetics, ketamine stimulates the cardiovascular system.

B True

C Surgery need not be cancelled for allergic or vasomotor rhinitis as long as the patient is clinically well.

D True

E True

3 Prevention of Nerve Injuries in the Anaesthetized Patient

A Axonotmesis is axonal and myelin loss within the intact connective tissue sheath.

B Most nerve injuries sustained during anaesthesia recover completely within a few weeks, though occasionally it may take months or even years.

C Men appear to be five times more vulnerable to ulnar nerve damage than women.

D True

E True

MCQs

4 Care and Monitoring of the Anaesthetized Patient

When a patient is under a general anaesthetic:

A ☐ Postoperative compartment syndrome can occur after prolonged hypotension with the legs in the Lloyd–Davies position

B ☐ A reduced core temperature decreases blood viscosity

C ☐ Lacrimation is a sign of light anaesthesia

D ☐ Automated alarm thresholds on monitoring equipment should vary with age

E ☐ For any transfer by ambulance, where there is a risk of cardiovascular instability, invasive arterial pressure monitoring is contraindicated because of the risk of dislodgement

5 Sources of Surgical Infection

In surgical patients:

A ☐ The neutrophil function may be enhanced by 25% after operation

B ☐ 75% of all nosocomial infections occur after operation

C ☐ The rise in nosocomial infections is related to the increased use of intravascular cannulas

D ☐ The rate of infection after shaving is ten times that seen after the use of depilatory cream

E ☐ Suprapubic catheterization has higher rates of bacteriuria than urethral catheterization

6 Antimicrobial Therapy

When prescribing antibiotics:

A ☐ All antibiotics are best absorbed on an empty stomach

B ☐ The combination of penicillin and tetracycline for the treatment of pneumococcal meningitis is superior to treatment with either antibiotic alone

C ☐ The use of the combination therapy of rifampicin and isoniazid in the treatment of *Mycobacterium tuberculosis* is clinically effective but runs the risk of increasing drug resistant strains

D ☐ The site of a vascular graft is immaterial as to which agent is most appropriate

E ☐ Prophylaxis is deemed appropriate for major compound trauma when there is exposure of bone

Core Module 1

4 Care and Monitoring of the Anaesthetized Patient

A True

B A reduced core temperature produces an increase in blood viscosity.

C True

D True

E When an anaesthetized patient with cardiovascular instability needs transfer by ambulance, invasive arterial monitoring is actually recommended because non-invasive blood pressure monitoring devices are too sensitive to movement artefact.

5 Sources of Surgical Infection

A The microbiocidal activity of neutrophils may be reduced by 25% after surgery.

B True

C True

D True

E Suprapubic catheterization has lower rates of bacteriuria than urethral catheterization, as well as better patient acceptability.

6 Antimicrobial Therapy

A Although most drugs are best absorbed on an empty stomach, others (e.g. doxycycline, itraconazole) are better absorbed with food.

B Treatment of pneumococcal meningitis with penicillin and tetracycline is inferior to treatment with either antibiotic alone. This is because the bacteriostatic action of tetracycline interferes with the bactericidal action of penicillin on dividing cells.

C By using the combination of rifampicin and isoniazid, the opportunity for drug-resistant strains to emerge is reduced significantly.

D For aortic grafts above the renal arteries, the blood supply to the kidneys may be compromised and therefore antibiotics used should not result in renal failure; in infrarenal reconstructions the kidneys should be spared, but the colon is at risk of ischaemia and translocation of bacteria can occur. Both these facts should be considered when choosing the most appropriate antibiotics for prophylaxis.

E Prophylaxis is inappropriate for major compound trauma when there is exposure of bone because this requires an active therapeutic regimen.

MCQs ⎯⎯⎯⎯⎯⎯⎯⎯⎯⎯⎯⎯

7 Asepsis, Antisepsis and Skin Preparation

When considering antisepsis and skin preparation before surgery:

A ☐ Frequent hand washing increases bacterial yield

B ☐ The application of 70% ethanol to hands has been shown to reduce viable organism counts by over 99%

C ☐ Alcohols are virucidal to HIV

D ☐ Chlorhexidine has poor skin adherence

E ☐ In newborn infants, absorption of iodine and iodophores has been reported as resulting in hypothyroidism

8 Day Case Surgery

Which of the following statements are true?

A ☐ A day case rate of 50% has been reported for laparoscopic cholecystecomy

B ☐ Patients undergoing laser prostatectomy with a postoperative catheter may be treated as a day case

C ☐ Postoperative complications and morbidity can be reduced by increasing the period of preoperative 'nil by mouth'

D ☐ Patients who are ASA grade 4 may not be treated as a day case

E ☐ The use of non-steroidal anti-inflammatory drugs (e.g. ketorolac) should be avoided in day cases because of their potential side-effects

9 HIV Disease and AIDS

Which of the following statements are true?

A ☐ HIV is highly mutagenic

B ☐ HIV infection leads to a dramatic increase in the number of CD4+ lymphocytes

C ☐ HIV is not directly oncogenic

D ☐ HIV is not contagious

E ☐ There is now clear evidence that insect vectors (e.g. mosquitoes) can transmit HIV

Core Module 1

7 Asepsis, Antisepsis and Skin Preparation

A True

B True

C True

D Chlorhexidine has good skin adherence and is persistent, thus exerting an antibacterial effect for over 6 hours after appropriate use.

E True

8 Day Case Surgery

A True

B True

C Specialist day surgery anaesthetists have discovered that postoperative morbidity can be reduced by *decreasing* the *nil per os* preoperative period for clear fluids from 4 hours to 2 hours.

D In specialist anaesthetic hands, some carefully selected ASA grade 4 patients may be treated safely as day cases.

E In day case surgery, the substitution of non-steroidal anti-inflammatory agents (e.g. ketorolac) for opiates has produced improvements in recent years.

9 HIV Disease and AIDS

A True

B Following infection with HIV there is an early and progressive derangement in CD4 cell function with a variable but inexorable fall in the number of CD4 cells.

C True

D True

E There is currently *no* evidence that insect vectors (e.g. mosquitoes) can transmit HIV. Furthermore, though saliva carries a potential risk of transmission, especially where mucosal injury is involved, there have been no documented cases.

MCQs

10 Drainage of Abscesses

In the management of abscesses:

A ☐ Haematogenous infection is common

B ☐ The main factor that determines the method of drainage is the size of the abscess

C ☐ After drainage, antiseptic dressing should be used routinely to pack the cavity

D ☐ Breast abscesses may be managed by aspiration and antibiotics

E ☐ Superficial abscesses are a recognized complication of endocarditis

11 Sutures, Ligature Materials and Staples

In wound closure:

A ☐ It is important to recognize that suture materials can be weakened by up to 50% at the knot

B ☐ Polydioxanone (*PDS*) retains its strength for only 10 days

C ☐ Polymers of glycolide and lactide are proteolysed and thus their disappearance is not entirely predictable

D ☐ Interrupted sutures should be sited so that each suture is half the thickness of the tissue being sutured away from its neighbouring suture

E ☐ Skin staples cause wound eversion

12 Surgery in Patients with Psychiatric Disorders

In patients with psychiatric disorders:

A ☐ Local anaesthetics with adrenaline appear to be safe with tricyclic antidepressants

B ☐ A potentially fatal type I reaction may occur with pethidine with monoamine oxidase inhibitors

C ☐ Schizophrenia is associated with a hypersensitivity to pain

D ☐ Neuroleptic agents slow peristalsis, thus causing ileus

E ☐ Delirium tremens is often associated and preceded by hyperkalaemia

10 Drainage of Abscesses

A Haematogenous infection is actually uncommon.

B The main factor that determines which method of drainage to use is the *location* of the abscess.

C Dressings soaked in antiseptics are not advantageous and may slow the healing process by damaging granulation tissue.

D True

E True

11 Sutures, Ligature Materials and Staples

A True

B Polydioxanone (*PDS*) remains strong in the tissues for a few weeks.

C Polymers of glycolide and lactide are hydrolysed not proteolysed, and thus their disappearance is much more predictable.

D In interrupted suturing each suture should be placed twice the thickness of the tissues apart and the distance from the edge of the wound should be the same as the thickness of the tissues.

E True

12 Surgery in Patients with Psychiatric Disorders

A True

B True

C Schizophrenia is often associated with pain insensitivity thus presenting a barrier to accurate preoperative diagnosis.

D True

E Delirium tremens is often preceded by hypokalaemia and so it is important to measure serum potassium levels before setting up a dextrose infusion.

MCQs

13 Anticoagulants, Corticosteroids and Immunosuppression

For patients about to undergo surgery:

A ☐ Any anticoagulation should be stopped and surgery delayed until the INR is below 2.5

B ☐ Heparin dosage should be monitored by means of the INR

C ☐ It is important to realize that, when nebulized, corticosteroids lose their mineralocorticoid effects

D ☐ It is essential that, for patients already on glucocorticoids, doses of glucocorticosteroids should be at least 200 mg/day to meet the demands of operative stress

E ☐ If he or she suffers from asthma, it is prudent to use nebulized β-blockers for the perioperative period

14 Perioperative Management: Cardiovascular Disease

In patients with cardiovascular disease:

A ☐ 75% of episodes of myocardial ischaemia may be silent

B ☐ Well-treated hypertension does not substantially increase the risk of surgery

C ☐ The presence of a third heart sound is associated with a 30% chance of postoperative pulmonary oedema

D ☐ Asymptomatic severe aortic regurgitation, even with a normal resting LV function, is associated with a very high risk of sudden death

E ☐ The resting ECG may be normal in up to 50% of patients with coronary artery disease

15 Perioperative Management of Respiratory Disease

For patients undergoing surgery:

A ☐ Vital capacity on the day after operation is reduced to 40% of the preoperative value

B ☐ Vital capacity reaches preoperative levels only after 7 days

C ☐ Volatile anaesthetics such as halothane are bronchoconstrictors

D ☐ Normal PEFR in adults is greater than 600 litre/minute

E ☐ Stopping smoking shows a beneficial drop in carboxyhaemoglobin within 1–24 hours

13 Anticoagulants, Corticosteroids and Immunosuppression

A True

B Any heparin use in the perioperative period should be monitored by means of the activated partial thromboplastin time (APTT).

C Inhaled or nebulized corticosteroids have the same mineralocorticoid effects as oral preparations.

D Seldom does the cortisol secretion rate exceed 200 mg/day and, even in response to major surgery, adults secrete only 75–150 mg/day. There is therefore no need for the exogenous dosage to exceed this level.

E No β-blockers should be used in asthma patients. However, it is wise to convert β-agonists to nebulizers during the perioperative period.

14 Perioperative Management: Cardiovascular Disease

A True

B True

C True

D Asymptomatic severe aortic regurgitation with normal resting LV function is probably a relatively benign condition. However, aortic and mitral stenosis carry a significant perioperative risk.

E True

15 Perioperative Management of Respiratory Disease

A True

B Vital capacity returns to preoperative levels only after 14 days.

C Halothane is a bronchodilator.

D True

E True

MCQs

16 Perioperative Management of Anaemia

In patients with anaemia:

A ☐ Each haemoglobin molecule has the potential to combine with eight molecules of oxygen to become fully saturated

B ☐ Oxygen extraction is improved by a shift in the oxyhaemoglobin curve to the left

C ☐ For those who refuse blood transfusion, oxygen consumption does not appear to fall until the haemoglobin level falls to less than 5g/dl

D ☐ There appears to be an increased risk of tumour recurrence in those who have been transfused

E ☐ Treatment with ferrous sulphate (200 mg t.d.s.) should result in a rise in haemoglobin levels of 1g/dl/week after 2 weeks

17 Perioperative Management of Diabetes

In management of patients with diabetes mellitus:

A ☐ The recommended diet should contain 60% of the total calorie input as carbohydrate

B ☐ Sulphonylureas such as chlorpropamide are especially useful in late pregnancy when other oral hypoglycaemics are contraindicated

C ☐ Focal mononeuropathies involving somatic nerves, such as the femoral nerve, often resolve in 18 months

D ☐ Patients with liver disease are prone to hypoglycaemia

E ☐ The use of Hartmann's solution in NIDDM is safe because it causes no significant alteration in blood glucose levels

18 Diathermy: Principle, Dangers and Precautions

When using diathermy:

A ☐ The frequency is considerably lower than that which would cause arrhythmias and fatal electrocution

B ☐ 'Cuttting' mode is produced with a continuous waveform

C ☐ In endoscopic work in the bladder, a conducting fluid is required

D ☐ Bipolar diathermy should not be used on appendages such as testes, penis or digits

E ☐ In patients with pacemakers, the pacemaker setting may be changed to a fixed rate

MCQs

16 Perioperative Management of Anaemia

A Each haemoglobin molecule can combine with four oxygen molecules to become fully saturated.

B Oxygen extraction is improved by a shift in the oxyhaemoglobin curve to the right.

C Oxygen consumption begins to fall when the haemoglobin reaches levels less than 8 g/dl.

D True

E True

17 Perioperative Management of Diabetes

A True

B Sulphonylureas should not be used in late pregnancy for fear of fetal hypoglycaemia.

C True

D True

E In patients with NIDDM an infusion of Hartmann's solution may cause a rise in blood glucose due to the lactate being used for gluconeogenesis.

18 Diathermy: Principle, Dangers and Precautions

A The frequency from the diathermy generator ranges from 20 kHz to 300 MHz, which is well *above* the threshold for fatal electrocution.

B True

C Diathermy does not work in conducting fluids because they short-circuit the current path, and therefore a non-conducting fluid such as glycine is used.

D Bipolar diathermy is safe on appendages but monopolar diathermy should not be used because it can cause thrombosis of end arteries.

E True

EMQs

19 Theme: The Use of Drains in General Surgery

A Pig-tail catheter

B Low-pressure suction drain

C Sump drainage

D Underwater seal drain

E Penrose drain

F Corrugated rubber drain

G Latex rubber T-tube

H Closed-tube drain

I No drain

For each of the clinical situations described below (1–3), select the most likely drain from the options listed above (A–I). Each option may be used once, more than once or not at all.

1 ☐ A 68-year-old male undergoing repair of a large incisional hernia

2 ☐ A 45-year-old female undergoing a routine, uneventful laparoscopic cholecystectomy

3 ☐ A 74-year-old male undergoing an anterior resection with the anastomosis well below the peritoneal reflection

20 Theme: Benign Skin Lesions

A Junctional naevus

B Compound naevus

C Seborrhoeic keratosis

D Kerato-acanthoma

E Cylindroma

F Pilar cyst

G Dermatofibroma

H Xanthelasma

For each of the clinical vignettes listed below (1–3), select the single most likely diagnosis from the options listed above (A–H). Each option may be used once, more than once or not at all.

1 ☐ An 85-year-old woman presents with a waxy papillomatous pigmented lesion on her trunk that has a friable hyperkeratotic surface.

2 ☐ A 60-year-old man presents with a rapidly growing nodule on his face that is elevated and has a central keratin plug.

3 ☐ A 28-year-old man presents with a smooth subcutaneous swelling on the scalp that is attached to the overlying dermis and is enlarging slowly.

EMQs

21 **Theme: Local and Regional Anaesthestic Techniques**

A Paravertebral blockade

B Interpleural blockade

C Intercostal blocks

D Femoral nerve block

E Sciatic block

F Neuraxial (spinal/epidural) block

G Local field infiltration

For each of the descriptions listed below (1–3), select the single most likely anaesthetic technique from the options listed above (A–G). Each option may be used once, more than once or not at all.

1 ☐ This gives ideal unilateral analgesia for a fractured femur.

2 ☐ These blocks are of benefit to patients with chronic post-thoracotomy pain because in 60% a single injection of local anaesthetic may provide effective relief for over 1 month.

3 ☐ This technique is particularly useful in infants (e.g. pyloromyotomy), in whom opioids may cause respiratory depression.

22 **Theme: Methods of Sterilization and Disinfection**

A Moist heat (high-vacuum autoclaves)

B Dry heat (hot-air ovens)

C Ethylene oxide

D Low-temperature steam and formaldehyde

E Glutaraldehyde

F Irradiation

G Boiling water

For each entry listed below (1–3), select the single most suitable form of sterilization or disinfection from the options listed above (A–G). Each option may be used once, more than once or not at all.

1 ☐ The regular in-hospital sterilization of flexible endoscopes

2 ☐ Wrapped surgical instruments

3 ☐ Industrial preparation of sterile products

Answers: 21 1D, 2A, 3G; **22** 1E, 2A, 3F

MCQs

1 Mechanisms of Pain

Which of the following statements are true?

A ☐ The results of highly selective peripheral nerve section for pain management show great promise

B ☐ Nerve injury results in the specific release of neurotransmitters in the ventral horn of the spinal cord

C ☐ Nerve injuries cause production of cholecystokinin within the spinal cord

D ☐ Patients with frontal lobe damage will not report pain spontaneously

E ☐ Pre-emptive analgesia is of no use in reducing the incidence of chronic pain

2 Perioperative Fluid Management

Which of the following statements are true?

A ☐ The microvascular endothelium separating interstitial fluid from the intravascular compartment is freely permeable to water

B ☐ The intracellular fluid volume is insensitive to changes in the sodium concentration of the extracellular fluid

C ☐ In patients with 'leaky capillaries' the oncotic pressure becomes increasingly important in determining fluid fluxes

D ☐ After intravenous administration of crystalloids the distribution of these fluids throughout the body depends on its osmotic activity

E ☐ 0.9% sodium chloride solution contains no free water and is thus restricted to the extracellular compartment

3 Metabolic Response to Surgery

Which of the following statements are true?

A ☐ The magnitude of the metabolic response is proportional to the severity of the surgical trauma

B ☐ A significant feature of the response to surgery is that cortisol release by the adrenal gland actively inhibits secretion of adrenocorticotrophic hormone (ACTH) by the pituitary

C ☐ There is failure of insulin secretion in response to the hyperglycaemia associated with surgical trauma

D ☐ Interleukin-6 is the principal cytokine released after routine surgery

E ☐ Plasma glutamine levels rise rapidly following surgery or injury

MCQs

1 Mechanisms of Pain

A Recent studies have shown that section of a peripheral nerve results in a number of changes that can act as a focus of pain. Therefore peripheral nerve section is seldom used for the management of pain, and indeed when used the results are often disappointing.

B Inflammation or nerve injury results in the release of neurotransmitters in the *dorsal* horn of the spinal cord and this is followed by activation of receptors which initiate a further cascade of events in neurones.

C True

D True

E Pre-emptive analgesia may well be important in reducing the incidence of chronic pain. Indeed a reduced painful input to the CNS at the time of surgery may be useful in reducing the incidence of chronic pain postoperatively.

2 Perioperative Fluid Management

A True

B Intracellular fluid volume *is* sensitive to changes in the sodium concentration (osmolarity) of the extracellular fluid, with hypernatraemia causing cell shrinkage and hyponatraemia causing cell swelling.

C Leaky capillaries result in the passage of colloid molecules through the microvascular endothelium to the extent that oncotic pressure becomes increasingly unimportant in determining fluid fluxes.

D After intravenous administration of crystalloids the distribution of these fluids is determined by their sodium concentration and they do not contribute to oncotic pressure.

E True

3 Metabolic Response to Surgery

A True

B A significant feature of the hormonal response to surgery is a failure of cortisol released by the adrenal gland to inhibit further output of ACTH by the pituitary. In a similar manner, hyperglycaemia fails to inhibit growth hormone secretion.

C True

D True

E Levels of plasma glutamine (an amino acid used by rapidly dividing cells) actually *decline* rapidly following surgery or injury.

MCQs

4 Wound Dehiscence and Incisional Hernia

For abdominal wounds:

A ☐ A burst abdomen carries a mortality of 15–30%

B ☐ Direct repair of an incisional hernia is possible if the defect is less than 2 cm in diameter

C ☐ A preoperative pneumoperitoneum before repair reduces the recurrence of an incisional hernia

D ☐ The Mayo technique of repair of incisional hernia is no longer recommended because of its high recurrence rate

E ☐ About 1% of patients undergoing conventional laparotomy develop incisional hernias

5 Classification of Wounds and their Management

When considering skin wounds:

A ☐ Wounds that are superficial to the interface between dermis and subdermal fat heal without granulation

B ☐ The use of absorbable sutures to close the dead space under the skin tends to increase the risk of poor scarring

C ☐ Staples lead to a significant diminution of the risk of poor scarring and cross hatching

D ☐ Paratenon will not accept split-skin grafts

E ☐ Regular massage of an itchy raised scar with a moisturizing cream is advised

6 Scars and Contractures – Grafts and Flaps

When dealing with skin wounds:

A ☐ The use of dissolving sutures improves the quality of the scar

B ☐ The currently optimal method of treating keloid is by excision and radiotherapy

C ☐ Storing split-skin grafts in tissue culture rather than in just a refrigerator maintains viability better

D ☐ The use of allogeneic skin requires that the antigenic epidermal component must be removed within 3 weeks

E ☐ The inclusion of the deep fascia significantly reduces the length-to-breadth ratio of skin flaps

4 Wound Dehiscence and Incisional Hernia

A True

B True

C Procedures such as lateral relieving incisions and preoperative pneumoperitoneum do not reduce the recurrence rate after incisional hernia repair.

D True

E About 11% of patients undergoing conventional laparotomy develop incisional hernias.

5 Classification of Wounds and their Management

A True

B True

C The use of staples for skin closure is actually associated with a higher risk of poor scarring and cross hatching.

D Paratenon will accept split-skin grafts, as will fascia, muscle, periosteum and perichondrium, but tendon, cartilage or cortical bone will not.

E True

6 Scars and Contractures – Grafts and Flaps

A The use of dissolving sutures avoids the need for suture removal but the quality of the scar produced may be reduced or impaired by the body process that dissolves the sutures.

B True

C True

D True

E The inclusion of the deep fascia with the cutaneous flap on the limbs actually increases their length to breadth ratio to 3:1.

MCQs

7 Immunocompromise and Opportunistic Infections

Which of the following statements are true?

A ☐ Gut ischaemia causing bacterial translocation can occur in patients on inotropic support

B ☐ Sterile food is being used increasingly in immunocompromised patients

C ☐ The diagnosis of CMV pneumonitis is made by transbronchial lung biopsy specimens

D ☐ *Pneumocystis carinii* is treated with oral co-trimoxazole

E ☐ The clinical presentation of *Toxoplasma gondii* is usually neurological

8 Blood Transfusion in Surgery

In patients undergoing surgery:

A ☐ The loss of 2,3-diphosphoglycerate (2,3-DPG) that occurs during cold storage of blood is regenerated rapidly after transfusion

B ☐ Postoperative transfusion is required when the haemoglobin level drops below 10 g/dl

C ☐ During massive blood transfusion the need for platelet therapy usually precedes the requirement for fresh frozen plasma (FFP)

D ☐ Albumin solutions are considered safe with regard to transmission of HIV

E ☐ Bacteraemias are the most common overall cause of documented transfusion-transmitted infection

9 Keloid

In patients with keloid formation:

A ☐ The incidence increases with age

B ☐ The keloid scar can become infected with a discharge of blood-stained pus

C ☐ Triamcinolone is specifically indicated in a 'great keloid former'

D ☐ The application of pressure diminishes keloid formation

E ☐ Postoperative irradiation only reduces the chance of keloid by less than 10%

MCQs

7 Immunocompromise and opportunistic Infections

A True

B Sterile food is *not* routinely used because it is expensive and unpalatable.

C True

D True

E True

8 Blood Transfusion in Surgery

A True

B Postoperatively, the need for transfusion when the haemoglobin level is 8–10 g/dl is controversial and recent trials suggest that transfusions may be unnecessary unless other clinical factors are relevant.

C True

D True

E True

9 Keloid

A Keloids are more common in young people aged 10–40 years and do not form in the elderly.

B True

C Triamcinolone is actually contraindicated in a 'great keloid former', because such keloids are usually best left untreated in order to avoid the formation of a new and often even more gruesome keloid.

D True

E True

Core Module 2

EMQs

10 Theme: Metabolic Response to Trauma

A Increase in body weight, normal sodium, potassium and nitrogen balance, normal urine output

B Slow increase in body weight, positive nitrogen balance, increased corticosteroid activity

C Rapid increase in body weight, negative potassium and positive nitrogen balance, negative fluid balance

D Sodium retention, excess loss of urinary potassium, catabolism of body fat, increased corticosteroid activity

E Reduction in body weight, normal sodium and potassium balance, positive nitrogen and fluid balance

F Reduction in body weight, negative sodium and fluid balance, positive potassium and nitrogen balance

For each of the body's phases of metabolic response to trauma described below (1–4), select the most likely combination of metabolic findings from the options listed above (A–F). Each option may be used once, more than once or not at all.

1 ☐ The injury phase of trauma

2 ☐ The period of fat anabolism

3 ☐ The 'turning point' in the metabolic response to trauma

4 ☐ The period of protein anabolism

11 Theme: Nutritional Support in Surgery

A Oral supplementation with liquid feeds

B Nasogastric intubation

C Fine-bore nasoduodenal intubation

D Cervical pharyngostomy

E Percutaneous endoscopic gastrostomy

F T-tube jejunostomy

G Peripheral intravenous catheter

H Tunnelled single-lumen central feeding line

For each of the clinical situations described below (1–3), select the most likely route for nutritional support from the options listed above (A–H). Each option may be used once, more than once or not at all.

1 ☐ A patient with neurogenic dysphagia secondary to a cerebrovascular accident

2 ☐ A patient requiring bowel rest for up to 14 days

3 ☐ A patient requiring enteral nutritional support for less than 4 weeks who has an increased risk of regurgitation or aspiration

12 Theme: Blood Transfusion

A Iron overload
B Febrile non-haemolytic reaction
C Post-transfusion purpura
D Haemolytic reaction
E Graft-versus-host reaction
F Hypocalcaemia
G Creutzfeldt–Jakob disease

For each of the transfusion situations described below (1–3), select the single most likely resulting complication from the options listed above (A–G). Each option may be used once, more than once or not at all.

1 ☐ A massive transfusion of cold blood

2 ☐ The erroneous transfusion of ABO incompatible blood

3 ☐ A transfusion of blood to a patient who has become sensitized to leucocyte antigens by previous transfusions

13 Theme: Dressings

A Conventional dressings (e.g. *Mepore)*
B Polyurethane dressings (e.g. *Opsite, Tegaderm, Bioclusive)*
C Hydrocolloid dressings (e.g. *Granuflex, Tegasorb, Comfeel)*
D Hydrogels (e.g. *Intrasite, Geliperm)*
E Osmotic agents (e.g. *Debrisan)*
F Alginates (e.g. *Kaltostat, Sorbsan)*
G Foams (e.g. *Lyofoam, Allevyn)*
H Edinburgh University solution of lime (EUSOL)

For each of the wound types listed below (1–3), select the single most appropriate dressing from the options listed above (A–H). Each option may be used once, more than once or not at all.

1 ☐ A deep, irregular, large cavitating wound

2 ☐ A wound with a significantly heavy exudate

3 ☐ A sutured wound on an irregular surface

MCQs

1 Management of the Airway and Acute Airway Obstruction

Which of the following statements are true?

A ☐ Stridor occurs on expiration

B ☐ In patients with a partially obstructed airway, ventilation via a bag and mask should use large tidal volume breaths while preparations are made for tracheal intubation

C ☐ The autonomic response to laryngoscopy and intubation may coincidentally be of value in patients with reduced intracranial compliance

D ☐ Blind nasal intubation may be performed in an unconscious patient who is breathing

E ☐ Auscultation of the axillae is the method of choice for absolutely excluding oesophageal intubation

2 Penetrating and Blunt Abdominal Trauma

Which of the following statements are true?

A ☐ Diagnostic peritoneal lavage is 98% sensitive for intraperitoneal bleeding

B ☐ A white blood cell count of 500/μl in a diagnostic peritoneal lavage is insignificant

C ☐ Rupture of a hollow viscus is easily missed on CT scanning

D ☐ The spleen is the most commonly injured organ in penetrating injuries to the abdomen

E ☐ Angiographic embolization may be required in cases of haemodynamic instability following fixation of pelvic fractures

3 The Pathophysiology of Fractures

In a fracture of the tibial shaft:

A ☐ A spiral fracture is produced by an indirect torsional force

B ☐ Surgical decompression for compartment syndrome should be undertaken if the difference between diastolic and compartment pressure rises above 30 mm Hg

C ☐ Compartment syndrome is more common in elderly patients

D ☐ Functional casts rely on the soft tissues (such as periosteum) to prevent shortening

E ☐ Callus formation should be clearly apparent on follow-up radiographs at 6–8 weeks

1 Management of the Airway and Acute Airway Obstruction

A Stridor actually occurs on inspiration and is usually indicative of obstruction at or above the level of the larynx.

B In patients with a partially obstructed airway, ventilation with a bag and mask should be undertaken, but large tidal volume breaths should be avoided because they may increase the pressure generated within the airway and air may be forced into the stomach, leading to regurgitation of gastric contents.

C In patients with a depressed level of consciousness and who have reduced intracranial compliance, autonomic responses to laryngoscopy and intubation may be deleterious. These reflexes may be blunted by using opioid drugs or anaesthetic induction agents with a muscle relaxant to facilitate intubation.

D True

E Auscultation of the axillae and epigastrium does not absolutely exclude oesophageal intubation.

2 Penetrating and Blunt Abdominal Trauma

A True

B A white blood cell count of $> 500/\mu l$ in a diagnostic peritoneal tap is considered significant, $< 100/\mu l$ insignificant, while $100–500/\mu l$ is equivocal.

C True

D The spleen is the most commonly injured organ in *blunt* abdominal trauma, while in penetrating injuries bowel perforation should be suspected.

E True

3 The Pathophysiology of Fractures

A True

B Surgical decompression should be undertaken if the difference between the diastolic blood pressure and the compartment pressure falls *below* 30 mm Hg.

C Compartment syndrome is more common in young patients.

D True

E True

Core Module 3

MCQs

4 Spontaneous Intracerebral Haemorrhage

Which of the following statements are true?

A ☐ Intracerebral haemorrhage is the most common type of stroke in patients under the age of 50 years

B ☐ Cerebrovascular amyloidosis is the second most common cause of intracerebral haemorrhage after hypertension

C ☐ Over the past 20 years the incidence of hypertensive intracerebral haemorrhage has risen dramatically

D ☐ After intracerebral haemorrhage the clinical deficit is maximal at presentation in over 80% of patients

E ☐ About 5% of patients present in coma

5 Assessment of Injured Patients

Which of the following statements are true?

A ☐ Needle cricothyroidotomy can adequately oxygenate a patient for half an hour

B ☐ Tension pneumothorax requires urgent positive-pressure ventilation

C ☐ Pulsus paradoxus is a well-recognized clinical finding in 'flail chest'

D ☐ Compensatory mechanisms can disguise a loss of up to 30% of circulating volume

E ☐ Patients with penetrating torso injuries may benefit from a delay in fluid replacement

6 Acute Spinal Cord Injury

In patients with acute spinal cord injury:

A ☐ Injury predominantly to one side of the cord (Brown–Séquard syndrome) causes motor loss on the contralateral side

B ☐ Oropharyngeal suction should not be carried out in the presence of bradycardia

C ☐ Anticoagulation in the form of warfarin should be commenced immediately after injury in the absence of contraindications

D ☐ Those with bilateral facet dislocation are more unstable than those with unifacet dislocations

E ☐ Decompressive laminectomy is known to increase the instability at the fracture site

4 Spontaneous Intracerebral Haemorrhage

A True

B True

C Over the past 20 years the incidence of hypertensive intracerebral haemorrhage has fallen dramatically, probably because of greater recognition and earlier treatment of hypertension.

D The deficit can be progressive over minutes to hours, though in about 30% the deficit is maximal at presentation.

E About 20% present in coma and this carries a very poor prognosis.

5 Assessment of Injured Patients

A True

B Tension pneumothorax does require urgent attention but with needle thoracocentesis and chest drain insertion. Positive-pressure ventilation is contraindicated because it will only make matters worse.

C Pulsus paradoxus is a well-recognized clinical finding in cases of cardiac tamponade but not flail chest.

D True

E True

6 Acute Spinal Cord Injury

A In the Brown–Séquard syndrome there is motor loss on the same side as the injury to the cord.

B True

C In the absence of contraindications such as head injury, anticoagulation should be commenced 24 hours after injury and initially should be in the form of heparin (500 units b.d.). After resolution of any ileus, full oral therapy with warfarin can be given.

D True

E True

MCQs

7 Injuries to the Cervical Spine

In the cervical spine:

A ☐ There is little inherent osseous stability in the lower vertebrae

B ☐ Unstable fractures are those in which late deformity is probable

C ☐ Full bony healing guarantees the recovery of stability

D ☐ The treatment of choice for rotational injuries is anterior fusion

E ☐ Flexion compression injuries causing burst fractures are associated with a high degree of cord damage

8 Early Management of Burns

Which of the following statements are true?

A ☐ With chemical powder burns, wounds must be kept as dry as possible until the patient reaches hospital

B ☐ Freeze-dried plasma is no longer used in resuscitation

C ☐ Nasogastric intubation increases the risk of bacterial translocation

D ☐ Damp dressings should be used on acute burns, especially in young children

E ☐ Hyperglycaemia is a well-recognized complication of early burns

9 Late Management of Burns

Which of the following statements are true?

A ☐ In an average patient, the upper limit for safe excision of life-threatening burns is 15% of body surface area

B ☐ An eschar is an excellent barrier to bacterial contamination

C ☐ The presence of *Enterococcus faecalis* is an absolute contraindication to skin grafting

D ☐ Meshed skin grafts should always be used on the hands

E ☐ Classical keloid tends to form 1–2 months after dermal damage

Core Module 3

7 Injuries to the Cervical Spine

A True

B True

C Bony healing of a cervical spine fracture does not guarantee the recovery of stability.

D The treatment of choice for rotational injuries of the cervical spine below C3 is posterior fusion with interspinous wiring following the reduction of the dislocation.

E True

8 Early Management of Burns

A In cases of chemical burns any powder should be brushed off the patient and then copious irrigation with water should be commenced and continued until the patient reaches hospital. Similarly, burns to the eyes should be irrigated with water to dilute the burning agent.

B True

C Nasogastric intubation in the burnt patient allows decompression of the stomach, and early enteral feeding is beneficial. This ensures that mucosal integrity is preserved, thus reducing the risk of bacterial translocation and endogenous infection.

D Damp dressings should not be used because they can lead to hypothermia, particularly in young children.

E True

9 Late Management of Burns

A True

B True

C Most patients are colonized by *Enterococcus faecalis* and, though pathogenic, this organism can be disregarded because most are removed by the excision of dead tissue, and therefore its presence is not an absolute contraindication to grafting, unlike the presence of β-haemolytic streptococci.

D A perforated or meshed graft is often the best choice where the bed oozes considerably, but sheet grafts should always be placed on the face and hands.

E Red, raised and itchy scars form in areas of dermal damage, usually 1–2 months after the wounds have healed. These hypertrophic scars are *not* keloid, because they fade and mature after about 18 months, leaving pale corrugated inelastic postburn scars.

MCQs ────────────────

10 Craniomaxillofacial Trauma

In patients with traumatic damage to the facial skeleton:

A ☐ Mid-facial damage can cause haemorrhage that can be so severe as to require external carotid artery ligation

B ☐ Primary surgery should not concentrate on aesthetic outcome – residual defects are best dealt with at a subsequent procedure

C ☐ Packing of the maxillary antrum is now an uncommon procedure

D ☐ Herniation of periorbital fat into the antrum can cause diplopia

E ☐ The open approach to fractures of the mandible should be via an external route

11 Immediate Care of the Burned Patient

When managing the burned patient:

A ☐ Clothing should not be removed for fear of pulling away adherent skin

B ☐ A period of 10 minutes' cooling should be followed by keeping the patient warm

C ☐ Full-thickness burns are usually painless

D ☐ The aim should be to keep the patient stabilized with a haematocrit of just over 0.45

E ☐ Application of silver sulphadiazine to a burn is strongly advised before transfer to a burns unit

12 Surgical Reconstruction of Mouth and Jaw

Which of the following statements are true?

A ☐ In the mouth, mucosa will grow to cover muscle used for reconstruction

B ☐ Temporalis muscle flap is particularly appropriate for reconstructing the soft palate and cheek

C ☐ The free radial forearm flap is less suitable than the pectoralis major myocutaneous flap for reconstructing the oral cavity

D ☐ Use of the radius in a radial forearm flap for jaw reconstruction is limited because only 40% of thickness should be transferred

E ☐ Jejunal flaps are particularly useful for oropharyngeal reconstruction

Core Module 3

10 Craniomaxillofacial Trauma

A True

B The best opportunity for a satisfactory aesthetic repair is at the time of primary surgery. Residual defects are difficult to correct subsequently and surgical outcome in these cases is often inadequate.

C True

D True

E Fractures of the mandible are best dealt with by open reduction and internal fixation, with the plates being applied through intra-oral incisions.

11 Immediate Care of the Burned Patient

A Any skin removed due to adherence to clothing after a burn is already dead and therefore the warning not to remove the clothes is groundless. In fact it is important to remove the clothing and cool for 10 minutes.

B True

C The often-repeated advice that full-thickness burns are painless is untrue.

D The patient should be well hydrated with a *low* haematocrit of about 0.35.

E The use of silver sulphadiazine is unnecessary prior to transfer and indeed confuses the picture because it makes assessment of the depth of the burn impossible on arrival at the burns unit.

12 Surgical Reconstruction of Mouth and Jaw

A True

B Temporalis muscle flaps are inappropriate for reconstruction of soft tissues such as the palate and cheek because the flap is denervated and will shrink and scar.

C The free radial forearm flap is more suitable than the pectoralis major myocutaneous flap because the thin and pliable skin of the flexor surface of the forearm conforms better to the contours and movements of the oral cavity than does the stiffer and thicker skin of the chest.

D True

E True

MCQS

13 Abdomen and Pelvis Injuries/Missile and Explosive Wounds

In the injured patient:

A ☐ Diagnostic peritoneal lavage is considered 98% sensitive for detecting intraperitoneal bleeding

B ☐ Exteriorization of a colonic repair is the treatment of choice for colonic injuries

C ☐ Splenorrhaphy is possible in about 50% of patients undergoing laparotomy for splenic trauma

D ☐ It is imperative, when debriding a wound, that all small metallic fragments are removed

E ☐ Missile and explosive wounds of the head and neck can be closed or reconstructed at the first operation

14 Intensive Care for Acute Head Injury

Which of the following statements are true?

A ☐ An intracranial pressure greater than 20–25 mm Hg is an appropriate threshold to initiate treatment

B ☐ All patients requiring mechanical ventilation for control of status epilepticus should receive neuromuscular blockade

C ☐ A reduction in mean arterial pressure can result in an autoregulatory reduction in intracranial pressure

D ☐ Sodium nitroprusside is valuable for controlling severe systemic hypertension in patients with head injuries

E ☐ Enteral feeding is preferred in head injury patients because it has a protective effect against gastric ulceration

15 Missile and Explosive Wounds

Which of the following statements are true?

A ☐ It is crucial to remove even the smallest metallic fragments from the wounds

B ☐ Fat can be generously excised

C ☐ Delayed wound closure should be delayed until significant fibrocytic activity has developed

D ☐ Some wounds of the head and neck can be reconstructed at the first operation

E ☐ The extent of tissue damage from missiles can be accurately assessed by the size of the entry and exit wounds

Core Module 3

13 Abdomen and Pelvis Injuries/Missile and Explosive Wounds

A True

B Exteriorization of a colonic repair appears to have few advocates currently. Injuries to the right colon tend to be treated by a right hemicolectomy, while injuries to the left colon are treated with a Hartmann's procedure or with primary closure if there are no signs of coexisting shock, peritonitis, major associated injuries or pre-existing medical conditions.

C True

D When debriding a wound, all foreign material must be removed with the exception of small metallic fragments. Attempts to find such small fragments are usually unsuccessful and make the wound unnecessarily large.

E True

14 Intensive Care for Acute Head Injury

A True

B Neuromuscular blockade should not be given to patients requiring mechanical ventilation for control of status epilepticus unless EEG monitoring is available to assess the presence of continuing epileptiform activity.

C A reduction in mean arterial pressure triggers an autoregulatory cerebral vasodilatation that increases cerebral blood volume and thus intracranial pressure.

D Sodium nitroprusside should not be used to treat severe hypertension because it also causes cerebral vasodilatation and an increase in intracranial pressure.

E True

15 Missile and Explosive Wounds

A In this type of injury all foreign material should be removed – with the exception of very small metallic fragments, because attempts to find them are usually unsuccessful and make the wound bigger.

B True

C Delayed wound closure should follow the exudative phase of wound healing (the first 2–3 days) and should *precede* fibrocytic activity (after 6–7 days) when the tissues become less flexible.

D True

E It is important to realize that the extent of tissue damage caused by missiles is not necessarily related to the size of the entry and exit wounds.

EMQs

16 Theme: Sepsis and Septic Shock

A Adult respiratory distress syndrome

B Septic shock

C Systemic inflammatory response syndrome

D Bacteraemia

E Multiple organ dysfunction syndrome

F Endotoxaemia

G Gram-negative septicaemia

For each of the definitions described below (1–3), select the most accurate term from the options listed above (A–G). Each option may be used once, more than once or not at all.

1 ☐ The presence of viable bacteria in the bloodstream

2 ☐ Sepsis associated with respiratory failure, renal failure, hepatic dysfunction and coagulopathy

3 ☐ Sepsis associated with hypotension, metabolic acidosis, oliguria and mental state changes

17 Theme: Organization of the Accident and Emergency Department

A Triage scale 1

B Triage scale 2

C Triage scale 3

D Triage scale 4

E Triage scale 5

For each of the clinical conditions described below (1–5), select the most likely UK National Triage Scale from the options listed above (A–E). Each option may be used once, more than once or not at all.

1 ☐ Knee pain for 6 months

2 ☐ Road traffic accident with multiple trauma

3 ☐ Fractured metacarpal of the hand

4 ☐ Fractured shaft of the femur

5 ☐ Supracondylar fracture in a child

EMQs

18 Theme: Head Injury

A 16-channel EEG

B Immediate transfer to a neurosurgical unit

C Skull radiography

D Blind immediate burr holes

E CT

F In-field intubation and ventilation

G Central venous line for CVP monitoring

H Intraventricular catheter placement under local anaesthetic for monitoring intracranial pressure

For each of the clinical situations described below (1–4), select the most likely initial procedure from the options listed above (A–H). Each option may be used once, more than once or not at all.

1 ☐ A 19-year-old man fell off his motorcycle and is comatose, with Glasgow coma score < 8 and loss of laryngeal reflexes.

2 ☐ A 45-year-old builder was hit on the head by scaffolding falling from a height. He is confused, with Glasgow coma score < 14 that persists after the initial assessment and resuscitation.

3 ☐ A 60-year-old victim of a violent assault has an open head wound and a depressed skull fracture.

4 ☐ A 23-year-old woman involved in a road traffic accident shows deterioration in level of consciousness of > 2 Glasgow coma scale points and progressive neurological deficit.

19 Theme: Late Management of Burns

A *Vaseline* gauze

B Silver sulphadiazine

C Early total excision and grafting

D Late debridement and grafting

E Multiple partial excision with repeated return visits to theatre

For each of the clinical scenarios described below (1–3), select the most likely treatment from the options listed above (A–E). Each option may be used once, more than once or not at all.

1 ☐ A deep dermal burn in an otherwise fit 45-year-old man

2 ☐ A-75-year-old woman patient with pre-existing respiratory failure exacerbated by smoke inhalation who has a full-thickness dermal burn

3 ☐ A 4-year-old child with a partial-thickness scald

MCQs

1 Brain Protection

Which of the following statements are true?

A ☐ Mannitol has a free radical scavenging effect

B ☐ Brain tissue has high levels of antioxidants

C ☐ Intracellular calcium is normally maintained at a higher level than extracellular levels

D ☐ Hypothermia of 30°C is used because it is not associated with cardiovascular and metabolic derangements

E ☐ Lactate production may enhance the production of free radicals

2 CT Imaging

Which of the following statements are true?

A ☐ It is possible to obtain CT images in an axial plane only

B ☐ Fat has a negative attenuation value compared to water

C ☐ Brain CT works best with a wide 'window' or range of grey-scale display

D ☐ Using spiral CT, an entire study can be performed during a single breath-hold

E ☐ Spiral CT is preferable to MRI in a woman of child-bearing age

3 MRI

Which of the following statements are true?

A ☐ MRI depends on the patient's body protons emitting their own radiowave signal

B ☐ Magnetic resonance's sensitivity to flow can be exploited to produce non-invasive angiography images

C ☐ Internal coils can show areas such as the prostate and anal canal in great detail

D ☐ Tissues such as dense bone are shown in unparalleled detail by MRI

E ☐ Pacemakers are absolute contraindications to MRI

MCQs

1 Brain Protection

A True

B Brain tissue has low levels of antioxidants but the advantage of administering free radical scavengers has yet to be established.

C Intracellular calcium levels are normally maintained at a lower level than extracellular calcium levels by means of homoeo static ionic pumps.

D Low temperatures of 30°C are associated with cardiovascular and metabolic derangements but mild hypothermia of 33–43°C is not and may prove beneficial to patients with head injuries and a Glasgow Coma Scale of 5–7.

E True

2 CT Imaging

A CT images are usually reconstructed in the axial plane but it is straightforward to obtain reconstructions in different planes with three dimensional reformats.

B True

C Brain CT works best with narrow windows (range of grey-scale display).

D True

E Alternative imaging techniques to CT scanning should be considered whenever possible in women of child-bearing age because of the high dose of radiation that CT requires. MRI or ultrasound may well be suitable.

3 MRI

A True

B True

C True

D Tissues containing low numbers of suitable hydrogen nucleii (e.g. aerated lung, dense bone) are poorly visualized by MRI, and CT scanning may be a better investigation in these areas.

E True

MCQs

4 Monitoring and Inotropes in the ICU

Which of the following statements are true?

A ☐ Spirometry is easily performed during mechanical ventilation

B ☐ Pulse oximetry should produce normal values of over 96% while breathing air

C ☐ A decreased delivery of blood to the lungs will cause an increase in the end tidal CO_2

D ☐ In a respiratory acidosis the base excess will increase

E ☐ High doses of dobutamine cause vasoconstriction

5 Minimally Invasive Thoracic Surgery

Which of the following statements are true?

A ☐ Valved ports are essential

B ☐ Double-lumen endobronchial intubation is required

C ☐ Minimally invasive thoracic surgery is contraindicated in neonates

D ☐ For a full exploratory thoracoscopy, the thoracoscope is best placed in the fourth intercostal space

E ☐ The left internal mammary artery can be anastomosed to the left anterior descending artery without cardiopulmonary bypass

6 Chest Wall Resection and Reconstruction

Which of the following statements are true?

A ☐ Surgical excision of a chest wall tumour requires lateral margins of clearance of at least 10 cm along the ribs

B ☐ Fascia lata harvested from the thigh has the advantage of becoming more rigid with time, thus providing the chest wall defect with increasing stability

C ☐ A transplanted resected rib inevitably necroses

D ☐ Free flaps are usually required for significant chest wall reconstruction

E ☐ Latissimus dorsi flaps may be pedicled on the thoracodorsal artery

Core Module 4

4 Monitoring and Inotropes in the ICU

A Spirometry is *not* performed easily during mechanical ventilation, though ventilators have pressure gauges that monitor proximal airways pressure during each respiratory cycle and this can be used to assess lung mechanics.

B True

C A decreased delivery of blood to the lungs will cause a decreased delivery of CO_2 to the lungs and result in a drop in the end tidal CO_2.

D True

E True

5 Minimally Invasive Thoracic Surgery

A In minimally invasive thoracic surgery, carbon dioxide insufflation and valved trocar ports are unnecessary.

B True

C Minimally invasive thoracic surgery is *not* contraindicated in neonates.

D In exploratory thoracoscopy, the thoracoscope is best placed low in the chest such as the seventh intercostal space in the mid-axillary line.

E True

6 Chest Wall Resection and Reconstruction

A Surgical clearance of primary chest wall tumours requires a skin margin of 2–5 cm, one uninvolved rib above and below the tumour, and lateral margins of 4 cm along the ribs, not 10 cm.

B Fascia lata harvested from the thigh tends to become flaccid with time and has a poor tolerance of infection.

C True

D Free flaps are not commonly required for chest wall reconstruction, because almost all of the major chest wall muscles may be mobilized and hence cover an extensive area when pedicled.

E True

MCQs

7 Ischaemic Preconditioning

Which of the following statements are true?

A ☐ Ischaemic preconditioning protects the heart against reperfusion arrhythmias

B ☐ The potent early protective phase of preconditioning lasts for 24 hours

C ☐ Increased collateral blood flow is thought to be responsible for early preconditioning protection

D ☐ Repeated balloon inflations have been shown to cause less ST segment elevation than the initial balloon inflation

E ☐ At the end of 10 minutes' ischaemic insult, preconditioned hearts have a significantly higher ATP content than controls

8 Nutritional Support in Surgery

When considering nutritional support:

A ☐ Patients with a body mass index (BMI) of 25 are malnourished

B ☐ Randomized trials in acute pancreatitis indicate that enteral feeding is associated with an outcome advantage

C ☐ Intermittent gastric/enteral feeding is associated with an increase in gastric and intestinal bacterial colonization

D ☐ Most patients require 0.5 g nitrogen/kg/24 hours

E ☐ Catheter salvage should not be attempted when *Candida* and *Staphylococcus aureus* infections are identified

9 Mechanisms Controlling Blood Flow and Arterial Pressure

In the control of arterial blood flow and pressure:

A ☐ The mean arterial blood pressure is equal to the difference between the systolic and diastolic pressure

B ☐ A 16-fold increase in perfusion pressure can be compensated for by halving the radius of the vessel

C ☐ An increase in production of lactate closes the Ca^{2+} channels, reducing the affinity of the myofilaments for Ca^{2+}

D ☐ An increase in arterial blood pressure causes the baroreceptors to effect a decrease in vagal tone

E ☐ The juxtaglomerular apparatus releases renin in response to reduced afferent arteriolar pressure

MCQs

7 Ischaemic Preconditioning

A True

B The early potent protective phase of preconditioning lasts for only 1 hour in most species.

C In the past, explanations such as the increased collateral blood flow and the induction of heat shock proteins were suggested for early preconditioning, but these have now been shown to be unrelated to it.

D True

E True

8 Nutritional Support in Surgery

A The normal BMI is 20–25 and adults with values of less than 19 are malnourished.

B True

C Intermittent feeding allows the gastric pH to fall and this may be helpful in reducing gastric and intestinal bacterial colonization.

D In the adult the provision of parenteral nutrition should not exceed 40 kcal/kg/24 hours and 0.3 g nitrogen/kg/24 hours.

E True

9 Mechanisms Controlling Blood Flow and Arterial Pressure

A The difference between the systolic and diastolic pressure is the pulse pressure, and because the heart spends roughly twice as long in diastole as in systole, the mean arterial blood pressure is empirically described as the diastolic pressure plus one-third of pulse pressure.

B True

C True

D An increase in arterial blood pressure causes a reflex decrease in sympathetic activity and increase in vagal tone to decrease cardiac output and total peripheral resistance.

E True

Core Module 4

MCQs

10 Cancrum Oris

In cases of cancrum oris:

A ☐ One of the earliest clinical features is severely diminished salivation

B ☐ 75% are seen in patients under the age of 10 years

C ☐ The majority are associated with vitamin E deficiency

D ☐ The mortality still remains over 50% despite improved diagnosis and appropriate antibiotic therapy

E ☐ The use of a nasogastric tube for feeding in children should be avoided because this interferes with swallowing

11 The Pleural Space

In surgery of the pleural space:

A ☐ A pleural effusion should always be aspirated immediately before thoracoscopy

B ☐ It is preferable to biopsy the visceral rather than the parietal pleura

C ☐ 70% of pneumothoraces occur in the absence of pre-existing lung disease

D ☐ The thoracoscopic approach to surgery for recurrent pneumothorax has significantly reduced the length of hospital stay

E ☐ Surgery is indicated only for secondary pneumothorax, in those patients who fail to respond to intercostal drainage

12 Shock

Which of the following statements are true?

A ☐ In shock the relative importance of oxygen in plasma decreases

B ☐ When blood loss exceeds 20% of blood volume, there is a marked vagally mediated bradycardia ·

C ☐ Vasoconstriction induced by haemorrhage is a uniform response throughout the body ·

D ☐ The onset of anaerobic metabolism is reflected by a decrease in the lactate/pyruvate ratio

E ☐ During the 'flow' phase of metabolism that follows prolonged shock, there is resistance to insulin activity

10 Cancrum Oris

A Among the earliest clinical features of cancrum oris is excessive salivation.

B True

C Many cases of cancrum oris in developing countries are associated with vitamin B deficiency.

D The mortality rate has improved dramatically with improved diagnosis and appropriate antibiotics from over 70% to less than 10% with some centres reporting a mortality as low as 5%.

E A nasogastric tube should be used for feeding in all cases where the lesion is so extensive that it interferes with swallowing. Such use will also prevent possible death from asphyxia or aspiration pneumonia.

11 The Pleural Space

A Thoracoscopy is facilitated if a pleural effusion is present and clinicians should be discouraged from draining the fluid immediately before surgical referral.

B Biopsy of the visceral pleura at thoracoscopy is not recommended but areas of abnormal parietal pleura should be biopsied.

C True

D A thoracoscopic approach to recurrent pneumothorax appears beneficial in terms of reduced postoperative pain, but there is no real reduction in hospital stay because discharge is usually governed by the time of chest drain removal.

E True

12 Shock

A In normal situations the oxygen carried in plasma is of little importance but in shocked states its importance increases when high inspired oxygen concentrations can be administered.

B True

C The vasoconstriction induced by haemorrhage is not uniform throughout the body but is more intense in tissues with a high ischaemic tolerance such as skin, while sparing the more vulnerable organs such as the heart, brain and gut.

D The onset of anaerobic metabolism is actually reflected by an increase in the lactate/pyruvate ratio. Indeed, lactate levels have been used as a marker of the severity of shock.

E True

EMQs _____

13 Theme: Conventional Radiography

A Gastrografin

B Thorium dioxide

C Effervescent granules

D Room air

E A combination of full-strength barium and air

F Filtered medical grade carbon dioxide

G Lower-density dilute suspension of barium

H Ionic water-soluble agent (e.g. urografin)

I Non-ionic water-soluble agent (e.g. omnipaque)

J Radiolabelled iodine

For each of the radiological investigations described below (1–3), select the most likely contrast agent from the options listed above (A–J). Each option may be used once, more than once or not at all.

1 ☐ Endoscopic retrograde cholangiopancreatography (ERCP)

2 ☐ Paediatric gastrointestinal studies

3 ☐ To achieve retrograde visualization of the portal vein and its branches during placement of a transjugular intrahepatic portosystemic shunt

14 Theme: Organization of Critical Care

A Glasgow Coma Scale 4	D APACHE II Score of 20
B Glasgow Coma Scale 8	E APACHE II Score of 25
C Glasgow Coma Scale 11	F APACHE II Score of 28

For each of the definitions described below (1 and 2), select the most likely 'score' from the options listed above (A–F). Each option may be used once, more than once or not at all.

1 ☐ A 25-year-old man was involved in a motor cycle accident. He was admitted as an emergency and was found to respond to painful stimuli with withdrawal and opening his eyes but with very garbled mumbling speech.

2 ☐ A 70-year-old, previously fit lady underwent emergency surgery for perforated diverticular disease. In the ITU she was found to have the following acute physiological measurements: temperature 38.8°C, mean arterial pressure 80 mm Hg, heart rate 110, respiratory rate 30, $Po_2 > 70$, arterial pH 7.45, serum sodium 138 mmol/litre, serum potassium 5.3 mmol/litre, serum creatine 1.8 mg/100 ml, haematocrit 48%, WBC 16/mm³.

EMQs

15 Theme: Complications of Infection

A Sepsis

B Multiple organ dysfunction syndrome (MODS)

C Systemic inflammatory response syndrome (SIRS)

D Septicaemia

E Compensatory anti-inflammatory response syndrome (CARS)

F Adult respiratory distress syndrome (ARDS)

For each of the clinical descriptions below (1-4), select the most appropriate descriptive terminology from the options listed above (A–F). Each option may be used once, more than once or not at all.

1 ☐ A fever of 37.5°C, a heart rate of 110 bpm, a respiratory rate of 20 breaths per minute, a $PaCO_2$ of 4.0 kPa, and a white blood cell count (WBC) of 15,000 per mm^3

2 ☐ A positive blood culture, a fever of 38.5°C, confusion, agitation, rigors and a blood pressure of 95/60

3 ☐ A fever of 35.5°C, a heart rate of 120 bpm, a respiratory rate of 30 breaths per minute, and a WBC of 3100 per mm^3

4 ☐ A state of inability to maintain homoeostasis with fever, hypermetabolism, anorexia, protein catabolism, altered fat, glucose and trace element mineral metabolism

16 Theme: Acid–Base Balance

A Acute respiratory acidosis

B Chronic respiratory acidosis

C Metabolic acidosis

D Acute respiratory alkalosis

E Chronic respiratory alkalosis

F Metabolic alkalosis

For each of the blood gas results described below (1–4), select the most likely acid–base state listed above (A–F). Each option may be used once, more than once or not at all.

1 ☐ A plasma bicarbonate of 18 mmol/litre and a pH of 7.2

2 ☐ A plasma bicarbonate of 29 mmol/litre and a pH of 7.3

3 ☐ A plasma bicarbonate of 22 mmol/litre and a pH of 7.6

4 ☐ A plasma bicarbonate of 38 mmol/litre and a pH of 7.55

MCQs

1 Cancer of the Pancreas

Which of the following statements are true?

A ☐ There is a clear-cut relationship between the incidence of pancreatic cancer and socioeconomic status

B ☐ The incidence of periampullary carcinoma is high in patients with familial adenomatous polyposis

C ☐ There is clear evidence of an increased risk of pancreatic cancer in patients with chronic pancreatitis

D ☐ Carcinoma of the uncinate process is often missed by endoscopic retrograde cholangiopancreatography (ERCP)

E ☐ Patients with an acute-phase response (i.e. C-reactive protein >10 mg/litre) have a potentially greater survival rate

2 Gastric Cancer

Which of the following statements are true?

A ☐ *Helicobacter pylori* depletes gastric juice ascorbic acid

B ☐ Genetic predisposition is limited to the diffuse type of gastric cancer

C ☐ Hypogammaglobulinaemia is associated with a 50-fold excess of gastric cancer

D ☐ The lymph nodes at the splenic hilum are N3 nodes for antral lesions

E ☐ The proportion of patients presenting in the UK with early disease (stage I) is less than 5%

3 Colorectal Cancer

Which of the following statements are true?

A ☐ Familial adenomatous polyposis accounts for less than 1% of all colorectal cancers

B ☐ Faecal occult blood testing has a high sensitivity for polyps

C ☐ The lateral resection clearance is more important than the length of distal resection margins in the development of local recurrence

D ☐ Recent trials using CEA levels to monitor follow-up have shown a survival advantage of over 10%

E ☐ Preoperative radiotherapy is associated with an increase in wound sepsis

1 Cancer of the Pancreas

A In the UK there is no evidence of a relationship between socioeconomic status, level of education or ethnic background and the risk of developing pancreatic cancer.

B True

C True

D True

E Patients *without* marked cachexia or an acute-phase response (i.e. C-reactive protein > 10 mg/litre) have a potentially greater survival rate.

2 Gastric Cancer

A True

B True

C True

D True

E Although the proportion of patients presenting with early gastric cancer (stage I) is lower than some countries like Japan, recent studies have shown that open-access endoscopy has improved this and currently it is about 15–25%.

3 Colorectal Cancer

A True

B Sensitivity of FOB testing is low as it fails to detect 20–50% of cancers and up to 80% of polyps.

C True

D Recent randomised trials using CEA levels for monitoring post-operative recurrence have failed to demonstrate any survival advantage.

E True

MCQs

4 Sarcomas of Bone

Which of the following statements are true?

A ☐ Chondrosarcoma usually occurs in middle age

B ☐ 50% of osteosarcomas occur around the knee

C ☐ Chemotherapy against micrometastases achieves cure rates of about 60–65%

D ☐ Extendible prostheses that can be lengthened are available for children

E ☐ In lung metastatic disease, repeated thoracotomy, metastasectomy and chemotherapy are usually recommended

5 Cutaneous Malignant Melanoma

In patients with malignant melanoma:

A ☐ The presence of multiple naevi is a strong risk factor

B ☐ Childhood sun exposure determines the lifetime risk

C ☐ When a metastasis is detected but the primary melanoma is unknown, the prognosis is, surprisingly, significantly better than in those patients where the primary is known

D ☐ About 25% of patients with systemic metastases survive 5 years after treatment

E ☐ Recurrence can occur as long as 20 years after apparently successful treatment

6 Informed Consent

When seeking informed consent:

A ☐ A patient with psychiatric illness or mental impairment is deemed automatically to be unable to give informed consent

B ☐ A 'tutor-dative' (court official) in England with appropriate authority can make medical decisions on behalf of a mentally incapacitated patient

C ☐ Children under 16 years of age may consent to a medical decision, provided they understand what it involves

D ☐ A screening blood test cannot be undertaken without the patient's consent

E ☐ Health Authorities may require evidence of the risk status of employees regarding hepatitis B

4 Sarcomas of Bone

A True

B True

C True

D True

E True

5 Cutaneous Malignant Melanoma

A True

B True

C When a patient presents with a metastasis and yet the primary melanoma is unknown, the survival is the same as if the metastasis had occurred after a known primary.

D Fewer than 5% of patients with systemic melanoma metastases survive 5 years.

E True

6 Informed Consent

A A patient with psychiatric illness or mental impairment does not necessarily lack the capacity to give informed consent.

B It is in Scotland that a 'tutor-dative' (court official) can make medical decisions on behalf of a mentally incapacitated patient, but elsewhere in the UK no one can carry out this function.

C True

D True

E True

MCQs

7 Metastatic Pathological Fractures

In patients with metastatic pathological fractures:

A ☐ Renal metastases are often cold on scintigraphy

B ☐ A significant perifracture haematoma seldom occurs

C ☐ Avulsion of the lesser tuberosity is an indication of imminent hip fracture

D ☐ At least 70% will unite after treatment with radiotherapy

E ☐ The spreading of tumour cells in the medulla by nailing a solitary renal metastasis is acceptable as long as the entire bone is included in postoperative radiotherapy

8 Mediastinal Tumours

In patients with mediastinal tumours:

A ☐ Germ cell tumours are the most common mediastinal tumours in children

B ☐ Stridor indicates tracheal compression of at least 75%

C ☐ Compression symptoms are twice as likely in children as in adults

D ☐ The optimal diagnostic test for a thymoma is percutaneous needle biopsy

E ☐ Thoracoscopy is particularly useful for posterior tumours

9 Anal Cancer

Which of the following statements are true?

A ☐ Anal canal tumours are now more common in women than in men

B ☐ Human papilloma virus type 16 can be identified from 80–90% of anal carcinomas

C ☐ The most common presentation is the patient's awareness of a perianal mass

D ☐ T_1 lesions at the anal margin are best treated by chemoradiation

E ☐ 50% of cases of synchronous inguinal lymphadenopathy are caused by inflammation

Core Module 5

7 Metastatic Pathological Fractures

A True

B True

C True

D Only about 30–40% of pathological fractures will unite even after radiotherapy.

E The spreading of tumour cells in the medulla by nailing is acceptable as long as the entire bone is included in postoperative radiotherapy *except* for cases of solitary renal metastases.

8 Mediastinal Tumours

A The most common mediastinal tumours in children are neurogenic tumours followed by lymphomas. Germ cell tumours occur in about 12% of patients of all ages.

B True

C True

D Diagnosing a thymoma at all on a very small biopsy may be impossible.

E True

9 Anal Cancer

A True

B True

C Only 25% of patients with anal cancer notice a perianal mass, but 50% present with pain and bleeding.

D T_1 lesions at the anal margin are best treated by local excision alone.

E True

EMQs

10 Theme: Soft Tissue Sarcomas

A Incisional biopsy

B Arteriography

C Ultrasonography

D Bone scan

E CT of the chest

F Fine-needle aspiration biopsy

G Excision biopsy

H Core-needle biopsy under local anaesthetic

For each of the clinical situations described below (1–3), select the most likely next investigation from the options listed above (A–H). Each option may be used once, more than once or not at all.

1 ☐ A 54-year-old woman has a proven rhabdomyosarcoma of the thigh that is under consideration for radical excision.

2 ☐ A 70-year-old man presents with a large, firm, painless swelling on the posterior aspect of his left leg that appears to be arising within muscle.

3 ☐ A 62-year-old man who had previously undergone excision of a soft tissue sarcoma from the chest wall presents with a nodule adjacent to the scar and a swelling within the axilla.

11 Theme: Cancer of the Lung

A Adenocarcinoma

B Spindle cell sarcoma

C Squamous cell carcinoma

D Bronchoalveolar cell carcinoma

E Clear cell carcinoma

F Giant cell tumour

G Secondary carcinoma

H Small cell carcinoma

For each of the tumour characteristics described below (1–4), select the most likely diagnosis from the options listed above (A–H). Each option may be used once, more than once or not at all.

1 ☐ This tumour is seldom seen in non-smokers but accounts for 40–70% of lung tumours and occurs in larger bronchi.

2 ☐ This tumour is very aggressive and pleomorphic with multinucleated cells and is often infiltrated with lymphocytes with a peripheral leucocytosis.

3 ☐ A tumour which is small and sharply delineated and behaves in a relatively benign manner.

4 ☐ Typically, this is a central submucosal endobronchial tumour with hilar enlargement and accounts for 20% of lung cancers. Paraneoplastic syndromes occur in 15% of patients.

EMQs

12 Theme: Research Study Design

A A double-blind study   **E** A before–after study

B A retrospective cohort study   **F** A crossover study

C A randomized controlled trial   **G** A historically controlled trial

D A controlled non-randomized trial

For each of the descriptions listed below (1–4), select the single most likely study design from the options listed above (A–G). Each option may be used once, more than once or not at all.

1 ☐ A prospective study in which patients receive different types of treatment by deliberate allocation or by observing naturally occurring variation in treatment between clinicians

2 ☐ A study with both prospective and retrospective components. Patients receiving a new treatment can be studied prospectively and their outcomes compared with retrospective data from patients who received control treatment

3 ☐ A study in which the treatment received within a trial is kept secret from patients, clinicians and researchers

4 ☐ A prospective study in which outcome measures are collected prior to and following treatment, with the patients acting as their own controls. There is no external comparison group

13 Theme: Biopsy Techniques

A Excisional biopsy   **D** Frozen section

B Incisional biopsy   **E** *Trucut* biopsy

C Fine-needle aspiration biopsy   **F** Radical resection with subsequent paraffin section

For each of the clinical scenarios described below (1–4), select the most appropriate initial biopsy technique from the options listed above
(A–F). Each option may be used once, more than once or not at all.

1 ☐ A solid solitary thyroid nodule that has produced follicular cells on fine-needle cytology

2 ☐ A potentially resectable mass in the head of the pancreas in a 71-year-old woman, but at laparotomy there is a firm lymph node found adjacent to the hepatic artery in the porta hepatis

3 ☐ A firm mass in the breast of a 45-year-old woman

4 ☐ A 56-year-old woman is explored with the suspected diagnosis of primary hyperparathyroidism and is found to have a nodule adjacent to the inferior thyroid artery, the exact nature of which the surgeon is unsure

MCQs

1 Dupuytren's Disease

Which of the following statements are true?

A ☐ The male:female ratio of Dupuytren's disease is 10:1

B ☐ There is clear evidence linking Dupuytren's disease with manual work

C ☐ Any single ray of the hand can be affected

D ☐ As the disease progresses, the nodules become more active and cellular

E ☐ Recurrence in the ray which was operated on occurs after about 30% of operations

2 Painful Conditions of the Shoulder

Which of the following statements are true?

A ☐ Most rotator cuff tears originate at the insertion of the supraspinatus tendon

B ☐ Exacerbation of impingement pain is usually produced by external rotation of the arm

C ☐ In rotator cuff tears, radiographs demonstrate that the distance between the superior surface of the humoral head and the undersurface of the acromion is usually greater than 8 mm

D ☐ In acute calcific tendonitis, the disease process is at its most painful when the calcium is being resorbed

E ☐ A ganglion arising from the acromioclavicular joint usually indicates rotator cuff disease

3 Fractures around the Knee

Which of the following statements are true?

A ☐ Isolated fractures of the femoral condyles are uncommon

B ☐ The force applied by the quadriceps can exceed the intrinsic strength of the patella

C ☐ Patients with minimally displaced fractures of the patella who can 'straight-leg raise' do not require a cylinder cast

D ☐ Wires used for external fixation can be safely placed to within 2 mm of the articular surface of the tibia

E ☐ If the depression is less than 4 mm in a type B2 fracture of the tibial plateau, the patient can be treated conservatively

System Module A

1 Dupuytren's Disease

A The prevalence of Dupuytren's disease in women is about half that of an age-matched male population and is not 10:1.

B There is no evidence that manual work predisposes to Dupuytren's disease, but there is evidence that a single episode of traumatic injury to the hand may cause the onset of Dupuytren's disease.

C True

D The nodules in Dupuytren's disease are gradually joined together by bands of fibrous tissue with low cellular density, and as the disease progresses the nodules involute and become less cellular.

E True

2 Painful Conditions of the Shoulder

A True

B Exacerbation of impingement pain in the shoulder is predominantly produced by internal rotation of the arm, not external rotation.

C In rotator cuff rupture, radiographs usually demonstrate that the distance between the superior surface of the humeral head and the undersurface of the acromion is *less* than 8mm.

D True

E True

3 Fractures around the Knee

A True

B True

C Patients with a minimally displaced fracture of the patella who can 'straight-leg raise' do not require operative treatment. Aspiration of the haematoma, application of ice and a compressive dressing reduces the swelling and then a cylinder cast should be applied and the patient mobilized, with weight bearing being encouraged. The cast can be removed after 3–6 weeks.

D Wires used for external fixation of fractures of the tibial plateau can be safely placed to within *5 mm* of the articular surface, not 2 mm.

E True

MCQs

4 Fractures of the Ankle

Which of the following statements are true?

A ☐ The integrity of the 'ring' at the ankle becomes unstable as soon as there is a single breach of the ligaments or bones

B ☐ Medial malleolus fractures alone are uncommon

C ☐ It is seldom necessary to repair isolated lateral collateral ligament injuries if bony congruity has been restored

D ☐ The temporary screw used for fixation of an unstable syndesmosis must be left *in situ* until full mobilization has occurred

E ☐ Use of a cast is essential for early mobilization of a fixed fracture

5 Club-foot

Which of the following statements are true?

A ☐ The male:female ratio is 4:1

B ☐ Once the deformity of club-foot has been corrected, the calf wasting will correct itself

C ☐ About two-thirds of children with club-foot require surgery

D ☐ If both equinus and varus deformities can be corrected to within 20°, the deformity is classified as mild or type I

E ☐ Measurements of radiographs are the most valuable predictors of outcome

6 Tendon Injuries of the Hand

Which of the following statements are true?

A ☐ In repair of flexor tendons, the placement of the core suture should be towards the dorsal aspect of the tendon ends

B ☐ In zone I, it is possible to excise up to 1 cm of flexor tendon without the risk of flexion deformity

C ☐ It is difficult to achieve a good result in zone II flexor tendon injuries

D ☐ In zone III, flexor tendons are flat in cross-section

E ☐ In mallet deformities with no evidence of a fracture on radiography, a mallet splint is applied and maintained continuously for 6 weeks

MCQs

4 Fractures of the Ankle

A The integrity of the 'ring' at the ankle will remain stable after a single breach of the ligaments or bone but two breaches will lead to instability and consequently incongruity.

B True

C True

D The screw of fixation for an unstable syndesmosis must be *removed* before full mobilization is permitted because the movement of the fibula during normal ankle function will lead to screw fatigue fracture.

E Use of a cast should be avoided in ankle fractures that have been fixed unless the quality of the bone is in doubt or the patient is unable to non-weight-bear or is unreliable.

5 Club-foot

A The male:female ratio for club-foot is 2:1 and not 4:1.

B After the deformity of club-foot has been corrected the calf wasting will remain, as will the limb shortening, and patients/parents should be warned of this.

C True

D If equinus and varus deformities can both be corrected to within 20°, the deformity is moderate of type II. Type I is when both equinus and varus deformities can be corrected to neutral.

E In follow-up studies it has been found that measurements of radiographs were of little predictive value, the only useful measurement being the calcaneus–fifth metatarsal angle on anteroposterior radiographs.

6 Tendon Injuries of the Hand

A In repair of flexor tendons it is recommended that the core suture is placed towards the volar aspect of the tendon ends to avoid the blood vessels that run longitudinally in the dorsal aspect of the tendon.

B True

C True

D In Zone III, both tendons are circular and not flat in cross-section.

E True

MCQs

7 Metatarsalgia in Adults

Which of the following statements are true?

A ☐ In a normal foot, the metatarsal heads lie in a straight line

B ☐ People who are flat-footed are more likely to develop metatarsalgia than those with high arches

C ☐ Hammer toes are flexed at the proximal interphalangeal joint

D ☐ Radiological evidence of a stress fracture of a metatarsal bone is more accurate in the early stages than a bone scan

E ☐ In a patient with Morton's metatarsalgia, the underlying neuroma should be removed

8 Fractures of the Shoulder and Humerus

Which of the following statements are true?

A ☐ The subacromial bursa lies beneath the rotator cuff muscles

B ☐ Anterior sternoclavicular dislocations are commonly associated with major visceral or vascular injuries

C ☐ After closed clavicular injury, shoulder pendulum activities should begin as early as the 7th day

D ☐ Recurrence of anterior dislocation of the shoulder is a relatively common complication

E ☐ Radial nerve palsy associated with a closed humeral fracture is an indication for immediate exploration

9 Acute and Chronic Osteomyelitis

Which of the following statements are true?

A ☐ The causative organism is *Staphylococcus aureus* in about 80% of cases

B ☐ Less than 5% of cases of acute osteomyelitis in the developed world become chronic

C ☐ Radiological changes in bone do not appear until 7–10 days after the onset of infection

D ☐ Ultrasound scanning is of more use than radiography in the diagnosis of suspected osteomyelitis

E ☐ The use of inert material as a temporary space-filler after debridement in chronic osteomyelitis (plombage) is being used with increasing enthusiasm

MCQs

7 Metatarsalgia in Adults

A True

B Patients with cavus feet (high arches) are more likely to suffer from metatarsalgia than those who are flat-footed with a low longitudinal arch.

C True

D In stress fractures of the metatarsals, radiographic evidence of a hairline fracture surrounded by callus may not be apparent for 3 weeks or more. Therefore a bone scan may be of more help in the early stages.

E True

8 Fractures of the Shoulder and Humerus

A The subacromial bursa actually lies *above* the rotator cuff muscles.

B Anterior sternoclavicular dislocations are seldom associated with major visceral or vascular injuries. However, posterior dislocations may be associated with occlusion of the superior vena cava or even the oesophagus.

C True

D True

E Primary radial nerve palsy associated with closed fractures of the humerus is not an indication for exploration because 95% of these patients will have recovered by 3 months.

9 Acute and Chronic Osteomyelitis

A True

B True

C True

D True

E True

System Module A

MCQs

10 Knee Replacement

Which of the following statements are true?

A ☐ In most normal activity, the medial compartment of the knee takes more of the load than the lateral side

B ☐ With increasing arthritic change in the knee, there is a progressive deformity exacerbating the natural valgus angulation

C ☐ In almost all currently successful knee replacement designs, it is essential that both the cruciate ligaments are retained

D ☐ In rheumatoid patients, it is crucial to perform an anterior synovectomy

E ☐ It is essential for all prosthetic components to be cemented in place

11 Forearm Fractures

Which of the following statements are true?

A ☐ Avulsion fractures of the olecranon seldom require surgery

B ☐ Children are seldom susceptible to compartment syndrome

C ☐ In elderly patients, in whom the check radiograph 1 week after a Colles' fracture shows displacement, remanipulation is of questionable benefit

D ☐ For fractures of the distal radius in children, there is a male to female ratio of about 4:1

E ☐ Rupture of the extensor pollicis longus usually occurs after a minimally displaced Colles' fracture

12 Acetabular Fractures

Which of the following statements are true?

A ☐ The advent of widespread availability of CT and MRI has rendered plain radiographs almost obsolete for acetabular fractures

B ☐ Undisplaced fractures are treated by a period of 4–6 weeks on skeletal traction

C ☐ Fractures of the anterior wall and column make up over 60% of displaced acetabular fractures

D ☐ Recovery is complete in 50% of patients with sciatic nerve palsy associated with acetabular fractures and posterior dislocation of the hip

E ☐ Heterotopic ossification can occur in 25–30% of cases of posterior or extensile approaches for displaced fractures of the acetabulum

System Module A

59

10 Knee Replacement

A True

B As the arthritic process in the knee progresses, the deformity increases with a *varus* angulation which reverses the 5–8° of natural valgus seen in the healthy joint.

C In virtually all currently successful knee replacements, the anterior cruciate ligament is discarded but it is essential that both the collateral ligaments are retained.

D In rheumatoid patients, some surgeons prefer to include an anterior synovectomy but this is of no proven value.

E Overall, total knee replacement is a reliable operation using modern designs based on the total condylar surface replacements concept and it probably does not matter whether the prosthesis is cemented in or not.

11 Forearm Fractures

A Avulsion fractures usually require surgical fixation because they disrupt the insertion of the triceps mechanism.

B Children are susceptible to compartment syndrome but it often goes unrecognized.

C True

D True

E True

12 Acetabular Fractures

A In spite of CT and MRI, high-quality radiographs are essential for acetabular fractures. Four views are required: antero-posterior view of the pelvis, antero-posterior view of the injured hip, an obturator oblique view and an iliac oblique view.

B Stable undisplaced fractures can be treated non-operatively by mobilization, partial weight-bearing on crutches, progressing to full weight-bearing at 6 weeks.

C It is fractures of the posterior wall and posterior column that make up over 60% of displaced acetabular fractures.

D True

E True

MCQs

13 Fractures of the Hip

Which of the following statements are true?

A ☐ The incidence of fractures of the hip is higher in caucasians than in blacks

B ☐ The blood supply to the femoral head is not significantly disrupted by extracapsular fractures

C ☐ Although cementing the stem improves survival, it increases thigh pain

D ☐ 7 years after hemiarthroplasty, 40% of patients experience hip or thigh pain caused by erosion or loosening

E ☐ In young adults, hip fractures are treated by emergency reduction and internal fixation

14 Rheumatological Disease

In rheumatological conditions:

A ☐ Inflammatory joint pain is worse at the end of the day

B ☐ Ageing cartilage is characterized by fewer collagen cross-links

C ☐ Obesity is strongly associated with osteoarthritis of the hip

D ☐ Pseudogout most commonly affects the knee

E ☐ *Helicobacter* has been implicated in the aetiopathogenesis of ankylosing spondylitis

15 Surgical Aspects of the Rheumatoid Cervical Spine

In patients with rheumatoid disease of the cervical spine:

A ☐ About 50% have neurological problems caused by atlanto-axial subluxation

B ☐ There is anterior horizontal subluxation, with the atlas and skull slipping forwards on the axis, when the transverse ligament is lax or ruptured

C ☐ Vertical translocation is secondary to rheumatoid erosions of the bodies of C1 and C2

D ☐ Fixation of the atlanto-axial complex is generally unsuccessful when performed from an anterior route

E ☐ Posterior decompression, whether at the atlanto-axial joint or subaxial spine, seldom requires a laminectomy

System Module A

MCQs

13 Fractures of the Hip

A True

B True

C Cementing the stem reduces thigh pain and improves survival.

D True

E True

14 Rheumatological Disease

A Inflammatory joint pain is worse on waking while mechanical joint pain is worse at the end of the day.

B Articular cartilage becomes thinner and stiffer with age and this stiffness is further increased by more collagen cross-links.

C Obesity is strongly associated with osteoarthritis of the knee (particularly in women) but not the hip.

D True

E *Klebsiella pneumoniae* has been implicated in the aetiopathogenesis of ankylosing spondylitis.

15 Surgical Aspects of the Rheumatoid Cervical Spine

A Only 15% of patients with rheumatoid disease have atlanto-axial subluxation, and of these 15% have a neurological problem.

B True

C Vertical translocation is secondary to rheumatoid erosions of the lateral masses of C1 and C2 causing the upper cervical spine to concertina on itself, and the odontoid peg can protrude through the foramen magnum.

D True

E Posterior decompression, whether at the atlanto-axial joint or subaxial spine, invariably requires a laminectomy.

System Module A

MCQs

16 Bone Transplantation

Which of the following statements are true?

A ☐ The most common source of bone allograft is the iliac crest

B ☐ Active preservation is essential for the success of chondral grafts

C ☐ Freeze-drying as a form of preservation should be avoided because it increases antigenicity

D ☐ Cancellous bone has poor osteoconductive properties

E ☐ Late development of infection in massive bone allografts is not thought to be related to the operation

17 Shoulder Instability, Fractures and Dislocations

With regard to the shoulder:

A ☐ Patients with atraumatic, multidirectional, bilateral, rehabilitation and inferior capsular shift (AMBRI) almost always require surgical correction

B ☐ The typical position for an anterior dislocation is with the arm in abduction and external rotation

C ☐ Disruption of the acromioclavicular joint is commonly seen in women between the ages of 65 and 89 years

D ☐ Fractures of the proximal metaphysis of the humerus show a dramatic increase after the age of 60 years

E ☐ Up to 10% of humeral fractures are complicated by non-union

18 Degenerative and Rheumatoid Arthritis/ Joint Replacement

In patients undergoing joint replacement:

A ☐ Uncemented acetabular components are still in widespread use

B ☐ Osteolysis occurs from the response of multinucleate cells to polyethylene wear debris

C ☐ Arthroplasty is of particular value in neuropathic joints (Charcot joints)

D ☐ Cement should never be applied under pressure because of the risk of embolization

E ☐ Deep venous thrombosis occurs in 5% of cases if sought on venography

MCQs

16 Bone Transplantation

A The most common source of bone allograft is the excised femoral head harvested at the time of total hip replacement. The iliac crest is the most common site for autografts.

B Chondral grafts are best used fresh and preservation actually carries a risk of damaging the graft.

C Freeze-drying actually reduces antigenicity but tends to reduce the graft strength.

D Cancellous bone has excellent osteo-inductive and osteoconductive properties and therefore tends to act as the 'split-skin' grafts of orthopaedics.

E True

17 Shoulder Instability, Fractures and Dislocations

A Patients with AMBRI should almost always be treated conservatively and surgery is required only in selected cases.

B True

C Disruption of the acromioclavicular joint is common and is typically seen in young men, usually following trauma or sporting injuries.

D True

E True

18 Degenerative and Rheumatoid Arthritis/Joint Replacement

A True

B True

C Neuropathic joints (Charcot joints) are a contraindication to joint arthroplasty.

D Cement is applied under pressure to prevent the entry of blood to the bone–cement surface, which would cause loosening.

E Deep venous thrombosis occurs in 40–50% of lower limb joint replacements if sought on venography, but clinically is seen in only about 3%.

System Module A

MCQs

19 Fractures of the Forearm and Hand

In fractures of the forearm and hand:

A ☐ A Monteggia fracture is a combination of a proximal ulnar fracture and a radial head dislocation

B ☐ Adult diaphyseal fractures are generally treated by open reduction and internal fixation

C ☐ In younger children, remodelling is better the further away the fracture is from the physis

D ☐ Undisplaced fractures of the phalangeal condyles are unstable and require splintage

E ☐ Most lunate fractures are secondary to Keinbock's disease

20 Fractures of the Hip

In patients with a fractured neck of femur:

A ☐ The anterior capsule is inserted half way down the neck

B ☐ The metaphyseal bone has such a rich blood supply that healing of an extracapsular fracture is not a problem

C ☐ After an intracapsular fracture about 75% of heads are viable

D ☐ The use of cement during arthroplasty increases postoperative pain

E ☐ Up to 40% are dead at 1 year

21 Fractures of the Tibial Shaft

In fractures of the tibial shaft:

A ☐ A simple transverse fracture is classified as an A3 type fracture

B ☐ Internal fixation should never be considered in an open fracture

C ☐ Lateral shift of 50% is compatible with normal limb function

D ☐ The use of external fixators is associated with a high incidence of delayed union and non-union

E ☐ Early weight-bearing increases the speed of union

MCQs

19 Fractures of the Forearm and Hand

A True

B True

C In younger children, remodelling of bone is better when the fracture is closer to the physis and when the deformity is in the plane of the primary movement of the joint.

D True

E True

20 Fractures of the Hip

A In the hip, the anterior capsule is inserted into the intertrochanteric line at the base of the femoral neck, while at the back it is inserted half way down the neck.

B True

C True

D The use of cement in arthroplasty may cause a slight increase in mortality from intraoperative cardiovascular problems, but it is associated with reduced postoperative pain, and earlier resumption of mobility.

E True

21 Fractures of the Tibial Shaft

A True

B Internal fixation, often using an intramedullary nail, may be indicated in type 1 or 2 open fractures if closed methods are likely to result in malunion. It is also indicated in juxta-articular fractures or following fascial decompression.

C True

D True

E True

MCQs

22 Fractures around the Knee

For fractures around the knee:

A ☐ A major vascular injury occurs in 2% of cases of supracondylar fractures

B ☐ Non-operative treatment is encouraged for almost all supracondylar fractures

C ☐ Patients should not bear weight until any supracondylar fracture has healed

D ☐ Post-traumatic osteoarthritis is seen in about 20% of undisplaced fractures of the tibial plateau

E ☐ 70–80% of patients with a fractured patella return to full function within 1 year

23 Soft Tissue Injuries

In the treatment and rehabilitation of soft tissue injuries:

A ☐ Myofibroblast contraction occurs towards the end of the inflammatory phase of wound healing

B ☐ Over-prolonged cooling produces a reactive vasoconstriction

C ☐ Manual application of hot packs is contraindicated when there is impaired sensation

D ☐ Ultrasound treatment should not be used over epiphyseal lines

E ☐ There is clear evidence that non-steroidal anti-inflammatory drugs (NSAIDs) hinder the healing process

24 Septic Arthritis and Osteomyelitis in Children

When considering septic arthritis and osteomyelitis in children:

A ☐ The metaphysis of the hip joint is intracapsular

B ☐ Differentiation between a Brodie's abscess and Ewing's sarcoma (malignant round cell tumour) may be possible only on histological examination

C ☐ The joint fluid in septic arthritis shows a marked increase in sugar content

D ☐ Bone scintigrams are incapable of differentiating infective from non-infective bone lesions

E ☐ The capsule should be left open after surgical drainage of the hip joint

22 Fractures around the Knee

A True

B Non-operative management of supracondylar fractures is demanding because the deforming forces of the muscles are difficult to overcome and anatomical reduction of the joint cannot be achieved.

C True

D Post-traumatic osteoarthritis is rare in undisplaced fractures of the tibial plateau, but if the fracture is displaced it occurs following 15% of lateral fractures, 20% of medial fractures and 40% of bicondylar fractures.

E True

23 Soft Tissue Injuries

A Myofibroblasts contract towards the end of the proliferation phase of soft tissue healing, resulting in contraction of the wound

B Cryotherapy to a soft tissue injury in the form of crushed ice in a wet towel or a cryocuff mechanism should be applied for only 15–20 minutes. Prolonged cooling produces a reactive vasodilatation.

C True

D True

E Suggestions that NSAIDs hinder the healing process have been unfounded, the reverse being more in evidence

24 Septic Arthritis and Osteomyelitis in Children

A True

B True

C In septic arthritis there is a marked reduction in joint fluid sugar content.

D True

E True

EMQs

25 Theme: Peripheral Nerve Disorders

A Leprosy

B Sarcoidosis

C Guillain–Barré syndrome

D Heavy metal poisoning

E Subacute combined degeneration of the cord

F Carpal tunnel syndrome

G Peripheral neuropathy

H Ulnar nerve entrapment

I Saturday night palsy

J Polyarteritis nodosa

For each of the clinical scenarios described below (1–3), select the most likely diagnosis from the options listed above (A–J). Each option may be used once, more than once or not at all.

1 ☐ An alcoholic who has neglected himself starts to develop a mixed picture of upper and lower motor neurone signs.

2 ☐ An immigrant female who has suffered from an upper respiratory tract infection starts to develop progressive and symmetrical ascending paralysis starting in the lower limbs with accompanying sensory loss.

3 ☐ A sheet-metal worker develops weakness of the grip and sensory loss over the ulnar aspects of the palm and the volar aspects of the 4th and 5th digits, with wasting and weakness of the small muscles of the hand.

26 Theme: Abnormalities of the Hip Joint

A Slipped upper femoral epiphysis

B Fractured neck of femur

C Perthe's disease

D Chondrolysis

E Congenital dislocation of the hip

F Haemarthrosis

For each of the clinical scenarios described below (1–4), select the most likely diagnosis from the options listed above (A–F). Each option may be used once, more than once or not at all.

1 ☐ A 15-year-old boy complains of pain in the upper leg and groin.

2 ☐ A 6-year-old boy living in a crowded inner city environment presents with a limp and hip pain. He is undernourished.

3 ☐ A 9-year-old Indian immigrant boy presents with a limp of insidious onset and a technetium-99m scintigram shows a 'cold' area in the region of the femoral epiphysis.

4 ☐ A patient who has previously undergone pinning of the femoral head presents with pain, stiffness and radiological loss of cartilage space.

Answers: 25 1E, 2C, 3H; 26 1A, 2C, 3C, 4D

EMQs

27 Theme: Common Disorders of the Foot and Ankle

A Hammer toe

B Mallet toe

C Claw toe

D Morton's neuroma

E Hallux valgus

F Hallux rigidus

G Plantar fasciitis

H Cavus foot

For each of the clinical scenarios listed below (1–4), select the single most likely diagnosis from the options listed above (A–H). Each option may be used once, more than once or not at all.

1 ☐ A slightly overweight, 25-year-old man who is a keen runner complains of marked pain in the heel on weight-bearing first thing in the morning. The pain tends to ease but returns later in the day with walking and standing.

2 ☐ A 58-year-old woman complains of pain when she walks, even when walking barefoot. There is pain on compression of the first metatarsal–phalangeal joint with limited dorsiflexion.

3 ☐ A 65-year-old woman complains of pain on walking on the tip of her second toe. A callosity is seen over the distal interphalangeal (DIP) joint and on the end of the toe which is flexed at the DIP joint only.

4 ☐ A 55-year-old woman presents with pain and paraesthesia radiating into the third and fourth toes. The pain is exacerbated by wearing tight shoes or squeezing the metatarsal heads.

28 Theme: Foot Injuries

A Fractured talus

B Fractured calcaneum

C Peritalar dislocation

D Transverse fracture of the fifth metatarsal

E Tarsometatarsal dislocation

F Phalangeal dislocation

For each of the traumatic scenarios described below (1–3), select the most likely injury from the options listed above (A–F). Each option may be used once, more than once or not at all.

1 ☐ A 20-year-old male athlete undergoing intensive training suddenly develops onset of pain in the foot.

2 ☐ A 50-year-old man fell off a ladder while trying to clean the gutter of his house. He landed heavily, feet first, suffering severe pain in his feet, and was found to have sustained similar injuries in both feet.

3 ☐ A 64-year-old woman was involved in a head-on collision while driving her car. Her foot was forcibly dorsiflexed against the pedal of the car, sustaining severe pain in the foot.

MCQs

1 Ischaemia Reperfusion Injury

Which of the following statements are true?

A ☐ The neutrophil is the prime mediator of reperfusion injury

B ☐ Oxygen free radicals delay tissue destruction by the oxidation of protein in cell membranes

C ☐ The myocardium suffers infarction after 17–20 minutes of ischaemia

D ☐ Rhabdomyolysis results in the release of glutamic-oxaloacetic transaminase

E ☐ Ischaemic preconditioning may result in up to 75% reduction in the extent of dog myocardial infarction

2 Surgical Management of the Spleen

Which of the following statements are true?

A ☐ There is considerable intersegmental arterial blood flow

B ☐ After splenectomy, IgA levels fall significantly

C ☐ Intrasplenic arterial adrenaline can result in a reduction in splenic size by up to 30%

D ☐ A partial splenectomy can be achieved by arterial embolization

E ☐ Overwhelming post-splenectomy sepsis occurs in about 20% of patients

3 Cerebrovascular Disease

Which of the following statements are true?

A ☐ Carotid bruits may occur without significant internal carotid artery stenosis

B ☐ A 45% reduction in diameter of the carotid artery on scanning represents a reduction in cross-sectional area of 90%

C ☐ Selective carotid angiography carries a risk of stroke of about 5–12%

D ☐ Subclavian steal syndrome can be corrected by a vertebro–subclavian bypass graft

E ☐ Pseudo-aneurysms are becoming more common following carotid endarterectomy

MCQs

System Module B

1 Ischaemic Reperfusion Injury

A True

B Free radicles cause tissue destruction by their interactions with lipids, nucleic acids and proteins. The oxidation of proteins in cell membranes can have serious consequences for membrane function.

C True

D True

E True

2 Surgical Management of the Spleen

A On entering the spleen, the arterial branches supply segments of splenic tissue, and there is little flow between segments.

B After splenectomy, IgM levels fall and take 4 years to return to normal, but IgA levels *rise* and IgG levels generally remain unaffected.

C True

D True

E After splenectomy the incidence of overwhelming post-splenectomy sepsis (OPSI) is only about 4% but the mortality rate is 50–75%.

3 Cerebrovascular Disease

A True

B A reduction in diameter of the carotid artery on Duplex scanning of 75%, not 45%, represents a reduction in cross-sectional area of 90%.

C Selective carotid arteriography carries a stroke risk of about 0.5–2%, not 5–12%.

D Subclavian steal syndrome may be corrected by a carotid–subclavian bypass, using saphenous vein or a prosthetic graft, an endarterectomy or a bypass from the aortic arch.

E True

MCQs

4 Vascular Malformations

Which of the following statements are true?

A ☐ Large shunts produce a progressive decrease in cardiac output

B ☐ Limb hypertrophy can occur due to hypoxia of the osteoblasts

C ☐ Embolization is particularly suitable for multiple arteriovenous fistulas

D ☐ Elastic pressure bandaging should now be abandoned as therapy for vascular malformations

E ☐ Even early treatment in childhood cannot prevent the development of limb-length discrepancy

5 Medical Therapy of Peripheral Vascular Disease

Which of the following statements are true?

A ☐ 50% of claudicants die of ischaemic heart disease

B ☐ Plasma fibrinogen is a poor predictor of graft occlusion in claudicants

C ☐ Thrombolytic therapy carries a 2% risk of stroke

D ☐ Transthoracic echocardiography is more sensitive than transoesophageal echocardiography

E ☐ Homocysteinaemia increases the thrombotic risk in adults

6 Vascular Injury

Which of the following statements are true?

A ☐ Persistent pulses are present in up to 25% of arterial injuries

B ☐ A loss of up to 2 cm in length of artery may be dealt with by adequate mobilization of the vessel and end-to-end anastomosis

C ☐ Almost complete recovery of muscle function can be anticipated after total ischaemia of up to 12 hours

D ☐ Long-standing false aneurysms with extensive intraluminal thrombus are best treated conservatively

E ☐ A severed limb may be stored in ice in a sterile plastic bag for up to 24 hours

4 Vascular Malformations

A Large shunts produce a progressive increase in cardiac output which may in itself lead to cardiac failure.

B True

C True

D True

E Early treatment in childhood can in fact prevent the development of limb-length discrepancy and good long-term results can be achieved with a combination of length correction and vascular surgery.

5 Medical Therapy of Peripheral Vascular Disease

A True

B Measurement of plasma fibrinogen is a strong predictor of mortality and graft occlusion in claudicants.

C True

D Transoesophageal echocardiography is actually more sensitive than transthoracic echocardiography.

E True

6 Vascular Injury

A True

B True

C Substantial recovery of muscle function can be anticipated if total ischaemia does not exceed 6 hours, but after this time recovery falls off. After 12 hours of total ischaemia, recovery is minimal.

D Long-standing false aneurysms usually containing extensive thrombus, are best treated surgically because compression may give rise to distal embolization.

E True

MCQs

7 Vein Harvesting

Which of the following statements are true?

A ☐ Before endoscopic harvesting, Duplex scanning should be used to mark out the vein

B ☐ Diathermy should never be used to achieve subcutaneous haemostasis during endoscopic harvesting

C ☐ Electron microscopy shows more trauma to the conduit after endoscopic harvesting than after open harvesting

D ☐ Using the minimally invasive vein harvester (the *Subcu-Dissector*) in a femorodistal bypass procedure, four incisions are usually required

E ☐ The minimally invasive approach has the distinct advantage of shortening the operating time

8 Venous Insufficiency

In the investigation of venous insufficiency:

A ☐ Continuous-wave Doppler ultrasound probes are not reliable in distinguishing deep and superficial venous insufficiency in the popliteal fossa

B ☐ Up to 50% of patients with liposclerotic skin changes at the ankle have venous incompetence confined to the superficial veins

C ☐ Descending phlebography in patients with deep vein incompetence may demonstrate retrograde flow extending from the femoral vein down to the knee or beyond

D ☐ The patient lies on a couch in a Trendelenburg position for Duplex ultrasonography of the venous system

E ☐ The foot venous pressure in a normal limb should fall to about 80–100 mm Hg on walking

9 Arterial Disease

In the investigation of arterial disease:

A ☐ Continuous-wave ultrasound is particularly useful at controlling the depth from which signals are returning

B ☐ A major advantage of spiral CT scanning is its ability to obtain images of a vessel in 3D

C ☐ Only 50% of patients with neck bruits have a significant internal carotid artery stenosis

D ☐ An ankle/brachial pressure index (ABPI) of less than 0.5 is usually associated with critical ischaemia

E ☐ Digital subtraction angiography is superior to dependent Doppler examination for demonstrating distal run-off vessels in critical ischaemia

7 Vein Harvesting

A True

B Main venous tributaries are divided between clips which can be applied endoscopically. However, further haemostasis can be achieved using diathermy.

C Electron microscopy studies have failed to show excessive trauma to the conduit and no evidence of injury at the site of tributary division when endoscopic harvesting is compared to the traditional open method.

D True

E Currently the only drawbacks to the minimally invasive technique are the cost of the equipment and the prolongation of the operating time. However, the time taken does diminish with experience.

8 Venous Insufficiency

A True

B True

C True

D For Duplex ultrasonography assessment of venous insufficiency the patient stands on a platform about 10–15 cm above the ground, taking the weight on the contralateral limb to that under investigation. The examiner sits on a chair with adjustable height to assist examination of the entire length of the leg.

E In a normal limb the foot vein pressure on standing should fall from 80–100 mm Hg at rest to 20 mm Hg or less on walking and rise back to the resting level over a period of 20 seconds or more simple standing.

9 Arterial Disease

A One of the disadvantages of continuous wave ultrasound is that there is no control over the area of tissue that is examined, because signals will be produced by any waves that are intercepted by the receiving crystal. The solution to this problem is pulsed ultrasound, opening the receiver only when signals from a predetermined depth are returning.

B True

C True

D True

E Pulse-generated run-off and dependent Doppler assessment are superior to digital subtraction angiography for demonstrating distal run-off vessels in critical ischaemia because these patients tend to have multiple-level disease that prevents the radiographic contrast medium from reaching the distal vessels.

EMQs

10 Theme: Acute Ischaemia

A Percutaneous thrombolysis
B Surgical embolectomy
C Thrombectomy and patch angioplasty
D Bypass surgery
E Intraoperative thrombolysis
F Lumbar sympathectomy

For each of the clinical scenarios described below (1–3), select the most suitable line of management from the options listed above (A–F). Each option may be used once, more than once or not at all.

1 ☐ A 76-year-old man who had previously undergone an aortobifemoral graft presents with acute ischaemia of the left leg and clinically is found to have thrombosed the left limb of the graft.

2 ☐ A 79-year-old man who is known to have a popliteal aneurysm presents with sudden onset pain in the leg and limb ischaemia.

3 ☐ An 82-year-old man who has recently had a stroke and is in atrial fibrillation presents with severe acute limb ischaemia and no palpable femoral pulse, but no previous symptoms of peripheral ischaemia.

11 Theme: Aneurysms

A Insertion of intravenous access, cross-match blood and transfer to the operating theatre
B Immediate ultrasound scan
C Immediate arteriography
D Immediate CT scan
E Immediate endovascular stenting
F Transfer to the ICU and continuous monitoring

For each of the clinical situations described below (1-3), select the most appropriate initial line of action from the options listed above (A-F). Each option may be used once, more than once or not at all.

1 ☐ A 73-year-old obese man is admitted with a history suggestive of renal colic but his urine is clear and his intravenous urogram is normal. On the radiographs, however, there are some suggestive flecks of calcification in the area of the abdominal aorta and he is tender in the epigastrium, though no actual mass is palpable.

2 ☐ A 69-year-old man is admitted with back pain and is found to have a palpable aortic aneurysm. He is haemodynamically stable but his chest radiograph shows a widened mediastinum.

3 ☐ A 75-year-old previously fit man is admitted with abdominal pain going through to his back and is found to be shocked, with a blood pressure of 90/40 mm Hg. He has a tender pulsatile mass in the epigastrium.

12 Theme: The Diabetic Foot

A Regular podiatry
B Removal of callus
C Antibiotics
D Debridement and removal of all infected bone
E Urgent arteriography
F Amputation of the forefoot
G Below knee amputation

For each of the clinical situations described below (1–3), select the most appropriate initial line of action from the options listed above (A–G). Each option may be used once, more than once or not at all.

1 ☐ A 60-year-old man with known insulin dependent diabetes develops marked ulceration on the sole of his foot with associated osteomyelitis. He has no pulses below a very weak femoral pulse.

2 ☐ A 55-year-old diabetic man presents with an abscess in his foot with underlying osteomyelitis of the metatarsal head. There is associated cellulitis but his peripheral pulse is good.

3 ☐ A 50-year-old overweight diabetic woman is found to have a large callus over the head of the first metatarsal head but no open ulceration.

13 Theme: Varicose Veins

A No investigations
B Hand-held Doppler ultrasound probe
C Phlebography
D Duplex ultrasonography
E Plethysmography
F Digital subtraction angiography

For each of the clinical scenarios described below (1–4), select the most appropriate line of investigation from the options listed above (A–F). Each option may be used once, more than once or not at all.

1 ☐ A 45-year-old woman has developed marked primary varicose veins following her two pregnancies. She has marked varicosities in the distribution of the long saphenous vein that are apparently all controlled at the sapheno-femoral junction. There is no past history of any significance.

2 ☐ A 55-year-old woman presents with marked recurrent varicose veins. She has previously been subjected to bilateral groin exploration and stripping of the long saphenous vein 15 years previously. The veins appear to be controlled in the groin.

3 ☐ A 35-year-old woman presents with marked unilateral varicose veins that clinically are in the distribution of both the long and short saphenous veins of her left leg. She describes an episode of marked tenderness and swelling of that leg during pregnancy 10 years previously.

4 ☐ A 65-year-old woman presents with marked skin changes of lipodermatosclerosis, haemosiderosis, eczema and marked ulceration. There is need of a quantitative assessment of overall impairment of venous function.

Answers: 12 1E, 2D, 3B; **13** 1B, 2D, 3D, 4E

MCQs

1 Acute and Chronic Infections in Otolaryngology

Which of the following statements are true?

A ☐ When the eustachian tube is blocked the pressure in the middle ear becomes positive, causing pain

B ☐ Opportunistic infections of cholesteatoma seldom respond to antibiotics

C ☐ The clinical picture of suspected bacterial parotitis is usually a suppurative adenitis

D ☐ Most units would offer tonsillectomy to any patient who has had just one quinsy

E ☐ The preferred initial treatment option for infected branchial cysts is simple drainage and antibiotic therapy

2 Surgery to the Salivary Glands

Which of the following statements are true?

A ☐ Surgery is usually required for recurrent sialadenitis

B ☐ In the submandibular gland, 50% of neoplasms are malignant

C ☐ Adenoid cystic carcinoma occurs most commonly in the minor salivary glands

D ☐ Damage to the lingual nerve as it crosses over the submandibular duct causes ipsilateral paraesthesia and paralysis

E ☐ Sweating and redness over the parotid area on eating may occur to some degree in almost 50% of post-parotidectomy patients

3 Thyroidectomy and its Complications

In thyroidectomy:

A ☐ Subcutaneous heparin should be given routinely preoperatively to all patients

B ☐ A right non-recurrent laryngeal nerve occurs in about 1% of patients

C ☐ Damage to the external branch of the superior laryngeal nerve causes paralysis of the cricothyroid muscle

D ☐ Any anticipated recovery of a recurrent laryngeal nerve palsy will be complete by 3 months postoperatively

E ☐ All cases of bilateral recurrent laryngeal nerve palsy will require immediate tracheostomy

1 Acute and Chronic Infections in Otolaryngology

A When the eustachian tube becomes blocked the pressure in the middle ear actually becomes *negative* and the pain comes from the drum being stretched and pulled into the middle ear space.

B True

C True

D True

E True

2 Surgery to the Salivary Glands

A Attacks of recurrent sialadenitis should be treated conservatively and surgery is virtually never necessary.

B True

C True

D Damage to the lingual nerve results in numbness or paraesthesia of the ipsilateral tongue but *no* paralysis.

E True

3 Thyroidectomy and its Complications

A Neither prophylactic antibiotics nor subcutaneous heparin are given routinely to patients undergoing thyroidectomy.

B True

C True

D Any recurrent laryngeal nerve palsy should be observed for at least 6–9 months before being labelled as permanent, and recovery can occur even after 18 months.

E In some cases of bilateral recurrent nerve palsy, a tracheostomy may be required, but in many cases the cords become immobile and positioned midway between the normal and cadaveric positions. Phonation is lost but respiration is possible.

MCQs

4 Thyroid Carcinoma

For thyroid tumours:

A ☐ The incidence of malignancy in a solitary nodule in a child under 14 years of age may be as high as 50%

B ☐ There is an increased incidence of papillary carcinoma in iodine-deficient areas

C ☐ Frozen section is helpful for demonstrating capsule and vascular invasion of a follicular carcinoma

D ☐ Hurthle cell lesions behave like follicular carcinoma with regard to their imaging by radio-iodine

E ☐ Medullary carcinoma is familial in at least 80%

5 Thyrotoxicosis

With regard to thyrotoxicosis:

A ☐ Plummer's disease is associated with IgG type thyroid stimulating antibodies (TsAb)

B ☐ Propylthiouracil must be avoided in pregnant women

C ☐ After I^{131} administration, more than 50% of patients will develop hypothyroidism within 10 years

D ☐ Recurrent hyperthyroidism occurs in about 4% of patients undergoing surgery for Graves' disease

E ☐ Toxic multinodular goitre is best treated by I^{131}

6 Primary Hyperparathyroidism

Patients with hyperparathyroidism:

A ☐ Are more likely to be MEN II than MEN I

B ☐ May be asymptomatic in up to 80% of cases

C ☐ Have a raised intact parahormone level, which effectively excludes other causes of hypercalcaemia

D ☐ Who are asymptomatic will develop end-organ involvement within 5 years in 20% of cases

E ☐ Will have a dramatic long-term improvement of bone mineralization after parathyroidectomy

4 Thyroid Carcinoma

A True

B There is actually an increased incidence of papillary carcinoma in iodine-rich areas.

C Frozen section at the time of surgery may be helpful in cases of papillary carcinoma but it has little role to play in follicular carcinoma, particularly because of sampling error. Vascular and capsular invasion therefore depends on formal paraffin sections of the whole specimen.

D Hurthle cell lesions, though maintaining the ability to synthesize thyroglobulin, do not readily take up radio-iodine.

E In most cases medullary carcinoma is sporadic, but is familial in at least 20% of cases.

5 Thyrotoxicosis

A Plummer's disease is where one or more nodules in a long-standing multinodular goitre become autonomous and produce an excess of thyroid hormones. Graves' disease is associated with TsAb.

B Propylthiouracil is actually valuable in pregnant women with thyrotoxicosis because it crosses the placenta less readily than carbimazole.

C True

D True

E Although small toxic multinodular goitres may respond to I^{131}, the most appropriate current management for most toxic multinodular goitres is surgery.

6 Primary Hyperparathyroidism

A Hyperparathyroidism occurs in nearly all MEN-I patients, in about 30% of MEN-IIa and rarely in MEN-IIb cases.

B True

C True

D True

E Parathyroidectomy has an initial positive effect on bone mineralization but no long-term advantage.

MCQs

7 Acute Abdominal Pain in Children

Which of the following statements are true?

A ☐ A plain supine abdominal radiograph can be particularly useful in the pre-school child with acute abdominal pain and vomiting

B ☐ In children under 3 years of age, intussusception is more common than acute appendicitis

C ☐ In patients with an ileocolic intussusception, rectal examination reveals altered blood in only about 10% of cases

D ☐ Urinary tract infection is a common cause of acute abdominal pain in children

E ☐ About 10% of boys with testicular torsion present with abdominal or inguinal pain

8 Infantile Hypertrophic Pyloric Stenosis

Which of the following statements are true?

A ☐ Bottle-fed babies are more prone to pyloric stenosis

B ☐ Bile in the vomit excludes pyloric stenosis

C ☐ Persistent vomiting results ultimately in intracellular acidosis

D ☐ Balloon dilatation is ineffective in infantile pyloric stenosis

E ☐ Symptomatic pyloric sphincter incompetence is a common problem after pyloromyotomy

9 Oesophageal Atresia

Which of the following statements are true?

A ☐ Prenatal diagnosis may be achieved by fetal ultrasonography

B ☐ Over 80% of infants with a distal tracheo-oesophageal fistula have associated maternal hydramnios

C ☐ Contrast studies are essential to confirm the nature of the fistula

D ☐ In isolated oesophageal atresia with no tracheo-oesophageal fistula it is nearly always possible to join the ends together with an immediate anastomosis

E ☐ After surgical reconstruction of oesophageal atresia, 50% of the patients will have problems with gastro-oesophageal reflux

7 Acute Abdominal Pain in Children

A True

B True

C In cases of ileocolic intussusception, rectal examination reveals altered blood in more than 50% of infants.

D Urinary tract infections in children are actually an uncommon cause of abdominal pain, particularly in boys.

E True

8 Infantile Hypertrophic Pyloric Stenosis

A Bottle-fed babies, and those of blood group A, are less often affected by pyloric stenosis.

B The vomitus is typically not stained with bile but the presence of bile does not exclude pyloric stenosis.

C True

D True

E After pyloromyotomy, recurrence of stenosis does not occur and symptomatic pyloric sphincter incompetence is uncommon.

9 Oesophageal Atresia

A True

B Only 30% of infants with a distal tracheo-oesophageal fistula have the association of maternal hydramnios.

C The use of diagnostic radiopaque contrast studies is unnecessary and potentially hazardous because there is a possibility of aspiration during the examination.

D In cases of isolated oesophageal atresia the distance between the two oesophageal ends is usually too great to allow an immediate anastomosis to be performed.

E True

MCQs

10 Umbilical Abnormalities in Childhood

Which of the following statements are true?

A ☐ At about 10 weeks of gestation, the allantois develops into the urachus

B ☐ Umbilical polyps invariably respond to silver nitrate treatment

C ☐ Associated severe malformations occur in up to 50% of patients with exomphalos

D ☐ Gastroschisis almost invariably occurs to the right of the umbilical cord

E ☐ Incarceration of an umbilical hernia is exceptionally uncommon in childhood

11 Congenital Diaphragmatic Hernia

Which of the following statements are true?

A ☐ The left side is affected in about 85% of patients

B ☐ In congenital diaphragmatic hernia the surfactant system is dysfunctional

C ☐ Administration of dexamethasone to the mother is used to prevent neonatal respiratory distress syndrome following premature labour

D ☐ In patients with congenital diaphragmatic hernia, inspiratory pressures should be high to encourage expansion

E ☐ With modern treatment, over 90% of infants with congenital diaphragmatic hernia survive

12 Undescended Testis

Which of the following statements are true?

A ☐ Undescended testis affects about 30% of pre-term boys

B ☐ A retractile testis can be manipulated to the base of the scrotum and stays in position on release

C ☐ Testosterone levels fall throughout childhood

D ☐ There is clear correlation between age of orchidopexy and the later development of malignancy

E ☐ There is evidence of microscopic deterioration of gonocyte transformation from the age of 1 year

10 Umbilical Abnormalities in Childhood

A True

B Umbilical polyps do *not* respond to silver nitrate treatment and should be excised in continuity with a central core of umbilicus to identify other vitelline duct remnants.

C True

D True

E True

11 Congenital Diaphragmatic Hernia

A True

B True

C True

D In patients with congenital diaphragmatic hernia, inspiratory pressures should be low (< 30 cm H_2O) but with a reasonably high positive end-expiratory pressure (PEEP) to prevent alveolar collapse (4–6 cm H_2O).

E Even with modern treatment, 30–50% of infants with congenital diaphragmatic hernia do not survive.

12 Undescended Testis

A True

B True

C True

D There exists no clear evidence that relates the age of orchidopexy to the later development of malignancy.

E True

MCQs

13 Biliary Atresia and Congenital Biliary Abnormalities

Which of the following statements are true?

A ☐ In about 85% of cases of biliary atresia, obliteration occurs at the level of the insertion of the cystic duct

B ☐ Although used diagnostically, radionuclide scanning with iminodiacetic acid derivatives cannot distinguish biliary atresia from neonatal hepatitis

C ☐ Hepatobiliary ultrasound can always positively diagnose biliary atresia

D ☐ A common pancreatico-biliary channel is found in only about 10% of patients with choledochal cysts

E ☐ Malignant transformation occurs in more than 40% of patients with choledochal cysts that are left *in situ* and drained into the jejunum

14 Cleft Lip and Palate

In infants with a cleft lip and/or palate:

A ☐ The formation of a cleft lip is usually secondary to cleft palate formation

B ☐ The Pierre Robin sequence causes excess amniotic fluid to push the fetal chin down and the tongue up between the palatal shelves

C ☐ There is an increased frequency in oriental races compared to whites

D ☐ Glue ear is more common than in normal children

E ☐ Growth of the midface is normal in unrepaired clefts

15 Diagnosis and Treatment of Adrenal Tumours

In patients with adrenal tumours:

A ☐ ACTH independent Cushing's syndrome is usually caused by bilateral micronodular adrenal hyperplasia

B ☐ β-blockers may precipitate a hypertensive crisis with phaeochromocytomas

C ☐ Those with Conn's syndrome have a suppressed plasma renin activity

D ☐ A 3 cm nodule is more likely to be malignant in a 70-year-old patient than in a 30-year-old patient

E ☐ Clinical remission after adrenalectomy for Cushing's syndrome is reported as being over 90%

13 Biliary Atresia and Congenital Biliary Abnormalities

A In about 85% of cases of biliary atresia, the obliteration occurs at the level of the porta hepatis (type III).

B Radionuclide scanning using iminoacetic acid derivatives can discriminate between biliary atresia and neonatal hepatitis by demonstrating the absence of bile excretion in atresia.

C Ultrasound scanning helps to exclude other causes of obstructive jaundice but cannot positively diagnose atresia.

D A common pancreatico-biliary channel is found in about 80% of patients with a choledochal cyst.

E True

14 Cleft Lip and Palate

A The opposite is true – the formation of a cleft palate, where there is a cleft lip, is usually secondary to cleft lip formation.

B In the Pierre Robin sequence *insufficient* amniotic fluid within the fetal membrane is responsible for pushing the fetal chin down on the chest and the tongue up between the palatal shelves. This prevents shelf elevation and fusion, resulting in a cleft palate.

C True

D True

E True

15 Diagnosis and Treatment of Adrenal Tumours

A An adrenal adenoma is found in most adults with ACTH independent Cushing's syndrome (80%). Bilateral micronodular adrenal hyperplasia is an uncommon cause of Cushing's syndrome.

B True

C True

D The incidence of adrenal nodules increases with age. Therefore the risk that a 3 cm nodule in a 70-year-old patient is malignant is not as great as in a 30-year-old patient.

E True

EMQs

16 Theme: Head and Neck Lumps in Children

A Medial ectopic thyroid gland

B Thyroglossal cyst

C Meningocele

D Hygroma

E Muscular torticollis

F Ranula

G Branchial cyst

H An inclusion dermoid

For each of the clinical scenarios described below (1–3), select the single most likely diagnosis from the options listed above (A–H). Each option may be used once, more than once or not at all.

1 ☐ An infant presents with a posterior mid-line skin-covered transilluminable swelling that appears as a simple cavity on ultrasound.

2 ☐ A 3-year-old child presents with a mid-line cystic swelling that moves up on protruding the tongue.

3 ☐ A child presents with a mid-line subcutaneous swelling on the head that feels putty-like and does not transilluminate.

17 Theme: Paediatric Urology

A Polycystic disease

B Obstructed mega-ureter

C Ureterocele

D Ectopic ureters

E Posterior urethral valves

F Neuropathic bladder

G Vesico-ureteric reflux

H Pelviureteric junction obstruction

For each of the clinical scenarios described below (1–3), select the most likely diagnosis from the options listed above (A–H). Each option may be used once, more than once or not at all.

1 ☐ A child presents with abdominal pain, which is worse after an increased intake of fluid, and ultrasound shows a dilated renal pelvis.

2 ☐ A young girl presents with urinary incontinence and continuous dribbling of urine from the vagina.

3 ☐ On an antenatal scan, there is oligohydramnios, a thick-walled bladder and bilateral hydro-ureteronephrosis.

EMQs

18 Theme: Disorders of the Testis

A Orchitis

B Epididymo-orchitis

C Tumour of the testis

D Torsion of the testis

E Epididymal cyst

F Varicocele

G Hydrocele

H Haematocele

For each of the clinical vignettes listed below (1–3), select the single most likely diagnosis from the options listed above (A–H). Each option may be used once, more than once or not at all.

1 ☐ A previously fit 16-year-old patient presents with an acutely painful swollen testis. He has had occasional discomfort before, which has always resolved spontaneously.

2 ☐ A 25-year-old patient has been investigated for infertility and was found to have a swelling in the left side of his scrotum that feels like 'a bag of worms'.

3 ☐ A 35-year-old patient who had an orchidopexy when a child presents with a painless firm swelling of the testis.

19 Theme: Goitre

A Anaplastic carcinoma

B Multinodular goitre

C Plummer's syndrome

D Graves' disease

E Pendred's syndrome

F Colloid goitre

G Physiological goitre

H Thyroiditis

For each of the clinical scenarios described below (1–3), select the single most likely diagnosis from the options listed above (A–H). Each option may be used once, more than once or not at all.

1 ☐ A 72-year-old woman suffered with a long-standing goitre. Recently, however, she had developed weight loss and palpitations and was found to be in atrial fibrillation.

2 ☐ An 87-year-old woman had suffered from a slight goitre for some years but recently the gland had enlarged rapidly and become hard and fixed and associated with a hoarse voice.

3 ☐ A deaf-and-dumb brother and sister both presented with a smooth enlargement of the thyroid gland.

MCQs

1 The Status of Laparoscopic General Surgery

Which of the following statements are true?

A ☐ Deep sutures are required to close all entry ports of 5 mm and larger

B ☐ It is clear that routine intraoperative cholangiography helps avoid bile duct injury during laparoscopic cholecystectomy

C ☐ Less than 5% of patients with appendicitis in the UK are treated by laparoscopic appendicectomy

D ☐ Laparoscopic mesh repair of an inguinal hernia can be performed under local anaesthetic

E ☐ Small-calibre laparoscopes are available to pass down a Veress needle

2 Appendicitis

Which of the following statements are true?

A ☐ The presence of faecaliths doubles the incidence of gangrenous change in acute appendicitis

B ☐ Ultrasound screening in acute appendicitis has a high specificity

C ☐ Peritoneal and wound drains are of little use after appendicectomy

D ☐ In regional ileitis, appendicectomy should not be performed for fear of the risk of fistulation even when the caecum is apparently healthy

E ☐ A carcinoid tumour of the appendix that is 2 cm or more in size requires a formal right hemicolectomy

3 Gallbladder Stones

Which of the following statements are true?

A ☐ The diameter of the common bile duct as seen on ultrasonography should normally be less than 6 mm

B ☐ Fit patients with asymptomatic gallstones should undergo cholecystectomy to prevent the possibility of complications developing

C ☐ The full length of the cystic duct should always be dissected out at cholecystectomy to prevent a sump syndrome developing

D ☐ For effective dissolution therapy, gallstones must be radiopaque

E ☐ Cholecystectomy decreases the incidence of duodenogastric reflux

MCQs

1 The Status of Laparoscopic General Surgery

A Deep sutures are required only to close port entry sites that are 10 mm or more.

B There is no evidence that intraoperative cholangiography helps to avoid bile duct injury, though it may allow earlier identification of any such injury in some cases.

C True

D Open mesh repair of an inguinal hernia can be performed under local anaesthetic but laparoscopic mesh repair requires a general anaesthetic.

E True

2 Appendicitis

A True

B True

C True

D In regional ileitis, appendicectomy should be performed as long as the base of the appendix and the caecum are healthy.

E True

3 Gallbladder Stones

A True

B Patients with asymptomatic gallstones should be managed expectantly. There is no indication for surgery because most patients will remain asymptomatic.

C The full length of the cystic duct should *not* be dissected out because this may cause either direct damage to the common bile duct or indirect damage by interfering with its blood supply.

D For effective dissolution therapy, the gallstones must be radiolucent and small, preferably no greater than 1.5 cm, and associated with good gallbladder function.

E Cholecystectomy increases duodenogastric reflux which may cause epigastric discomfort and exacerbate any gastro-oesophageal reflux symptoms.

MCQs

4 Crohn's Disease of the Small Bowel

Which of the following statements are true?

A ☐ Patients with Crohn's disease seldom achieve a normal lifespan

B ☐ In duodenal Crohn's disease, gastrojejunal bypass is preferred to strictureplasty

C ☐ The most common indication for surgical intervention in small bowel Crohn's disease is recurrent intestinal colic

D ☐ Bleeding is an increasingly common presentation of small bowel Crohn's disease

E ☐ Strictureplasty is indicated for all strictures narrower than 30 mm

5 Benign and Malignant Liver Tumours

Which of the following statements are true?

A ☐ Focal nodular hyperplasia is a premalignant condition

B ☐ Over 90% of cases of hepatocellular carcinoma occur in patients with cirrhosis or hepatitis B or C

C ☐ Liver cell adenomas associated with the contraceptive pill may regress after withdrawal of the treatment

D ☐ Distant metastases from hepatocellular carcinoma are a late feature

E ☐ The fibrolamellar variant of hepatocellular carcinoma has a significantly worse prognosis

6 Portal Hypertension and Oesophagogastric Varices

Which of the following statements are true?

A ☐ About 30% of patients bleeding from varices die during their first in-patient episode

B ☐ Corrected portal pressure normally does not exceed 10 mm Hg

C ☐ In portal hypertension, the liver is deprived of many of its trophic factors

D ☐ Wedged hepatic vein pressure is reduced in sinusoidal portal hypertension

E ☐ Banding of varices is more suitable than sclerotherapy in acutely bleeding patients

4 Crohn's Disease of the Small Bowel

A Patients with Crohn's disease who are well managed usually have a normal lifespan but are likely to require medical management for 40–50 years.

B Wherever feasible, duodenal strictureplasty is preferred to gastrojejunal bypass because the latter procedure is associated with a high incidence of stomal ulceration, and the addition of a vagotomy can produce troublesome diarrhoea.

C True

D Neither bleeding nor free perforation appears to be a common presentation of small bowel Crohn's disease.

E The presence of strictures in the small bowel can be assessed by using a balloon catheter blown up to a diameter of 25 mm. Any stricture narrower than 20 mm should be subjected to a strictureplasty.

5 Benign and Malignant Liver Tumours

A Focal nodular hyperplasia is *not* thought to be premalignant, but liver cell adenoma is associated with a low malignant potential.

B True

C True

D True

E The fibrolamellar variant of hepatocellular carcinoma found in younger patients, usually women, with no evidence of cirrhosis or hepatitis infection, carries a significantly better prognosis after treatment.

6 Portal Hypertension and Oesophagogastric Varices

A True

B True

C True

D Transjugular access can be used to measure wedged hepatic vein pressure, which is *raised* in sinusoidal portal hypertension.

E The tunnel vision produced by the band application device on the tip of the endoscope can restrict visibility and thus render the technique less suitable for the acutely bleeding patient. However, trials have shown that banding can produce better control of bleeding than sclerotherapy.

MCQs

7 Investigation of the Biliary Tree and the Jaundiced Patient

Which of the following statements are true?

A ☐ Ultrasonography detects more than 90% of liver metastases

B ☐ Severe life-threatening acute pancreatitis occurs in about 30% of patients undergoing endoscopic retrograde cholangiopancreatography (ERCP)

C ☐ MRI is of particular value in patients with a non-dilated duct system

D ☐ ERCP provides reliable information about the state of the gallbladder

E ☐ CT is usually more accurate than ultrasonography in the delineation of an extrinsic malignant mass causing bile duct obstruction

8 Biliary Anatomical Abnormalities

Which of the following statements are true?

A ☐ Anomalies in biliary anatomy are seen in more than 50% of patients undergoing biliary surgery

B ☐ Ductal anomalies are more common in patients with cholelithiasis

C ☐ The confluence of the right and left hepatic ducts is intrahepatic in 40% of individuals

D ☐ The risk of malignant change in patients with choledochal cysts is removed after excision of the cyst

E ☐ In 36% of patients, the right hepatic artery arises from the superior mesenteric artery

9 Oesophageal Motility Disorders

Which of the following statements are true?

A ☐ Endoscopy provides reliable information about oesophageal muscular spasm

B ☐ Nutcracker oesophagus shows a grossly abnormal peristaltic morphology with normal amplitude

C ☐ There is usually loss of ganglion cells of Auerbach's plexus in achalasia

D ☐ Balloon dilatation produces symptomatic improvement in about 80% of cases of achalasia

E ☐ 24-hour pH manometry has shown a considerable correlation between symptoms and manometric abnormalities

7 Investigation of the Biliary Tree and the Jaundiced Patient

A True

B After ERCP, mild self-limiting pancreatitis occurs in about 3% of patients but more severe life-threatening pancreatitis in seen in only about 0.1% of patients.

C MRI scanning of the bile duct is improving all the time but in early series there were occasional problems in routinely depicting non-dilated bile ducts.

D ERCP is not reliably useful for investigating the gallbladder, which may be difficult to fill because of a tortuous cystic duct, oedema or even a stone in Hartmann's pouch.

E True

8 Biliary Anatomical Abnormalities

A True

B True

C The confluence of the right and left hepatic ducts is extrahepatic in 94% of individuals.

D Patients with choledochal cysts remain at risk of cholangiocarcinoma at other sites, even after excision, and therefore should undergo life-long follow-up.

E The right hepatic artery arises from the superior mesenteric artery in about 16% of patients and then runs up in a groove between the common hepatic duct and the portal vein.

9 Oesophageal Motility Disorders

A Muscular spasm seen at endoscopy is a very unreliable sign.

B In 'nutcracker oesophagus', manometry studies show normal peristaltic morphology but an abnormally high amplitude of greater than 180 mm Hg.

C True

D True

E 24-hour pH monitoring in achalasia should be interpreted with very great care and there is no simple correlation between symptoms and manometric abnormalities.

MCQs

10 Perforations of the Oesophagus

Which of the following statements are true?

A ☐ Patients who sustain a spontaneous perforation of the oesophagus usually have an antecedent oesophageal disease

B ☐ A spontaneous rupture usually occurs on the right side

C ☐ A repair of a rupture in the lower few centimetres of the oesophagus should be covered by a total fundoplication

D ☐ Most fistulas following attempted repair of a spontaneous rupture of the oesophagus heal eventually

E ☐ Instrumentation perforation of the oesophagus usually responds to non-operative treatment

11 Presentation and Management of Peptic Ulceration

Which of the following statements are true?

A ☐ The male:female ratio for duodenal ulceration is decreasing progressively

B ☐ Up to 96% of duodenal ulcers are associated with *Helicobacter pylori* infection

C ☐ Type III gastric ulcers tend to have low acid secretion

D ☐ The recurrence rate for duodenal ulcers after *Helicobacter pylori* eradication is less than 10%

E ☐ A giant gastric ulcer (> 3 cm) is an absolute indication for surgery in itself

12 Complications of Peptic Ulceration

Which of the following statements are true?

A ☐ The mortality rate from peptic ulcer haemorrhage has remained unchanged over the last 50 years

B ☐ A pneumoperitoneum is visible on an upright chest radiograph in 80% of patients with peptic ulcer perforation

C ☐ Recurrent peptic ulceration after proximal gastric vagotomy is about 5%

D ☐ Subcutaneous injection of octreotide is of proven benefit in early dumping

E ☐ The risk of gastric remnant carcinoma is greatest following Billroth II gastrectomy

MCQs

10 Perforations of the Oesophagus

A Patients who sustain a spontaneous perforation of the oesophagus usually do *not* have any antecedent oesophageal disease.

B A spontaneous rupture of the oesophagus usually occurs on the *left* side in the lower third.

C True

D True

E True

11 Presentation and Management of Peptic Ulceration

A True

B True

C Type III (prepyloric) ulcers tend to have a high acid secretion but for some unknown reason have a poor response after proximal gastric vagotomy.

D True

E A giant gastric ulcer (> 3cm) should not be seen in itself as an indication for surgery. However, the possibility of carcinoma within a gastric ulcer should always be considered and any non-healing gastric ulcer should be excised.

12 Complications of Peptic Ulceration

A True

B True

C Recurrent peptic ulceration is seen in about 25% of patients after proximal gastric vagotomy, in 3–9% after truncal vagotomy and drainage, and in about 0.5% after truncal vagotomy and antrectomy.

D True

E True

MCQs

13 Faecal Incontinence

Which of the following statements are true?

A ☐ It is estimated that the prevalence of faecal incontinence is more than 1% in the over-65 age group

B ☐ At rest the external sphincter contributes 60% of the resting tone

C ☐ Numerically, the most common cause of incontinence is faecal impaction

D ☐ Patients with higher spinal defects tend to have better function than those with lower defects

E ☐ Repair of direct sphincter injuries is successful in only about 20–30% of patients

14 Colonic Haemorrhage

Which of the following statements are true?

A ☐ In the UK, acute colonic bleeding makes up only 5% of hospital admissions for gastrointestinal haemorrhage

B ☐ Re-bleeding from right-sided colonic diverticula occurs in 80–90% of patients

C ☐ Colorectal carcinomas seldom present with an acute brisk haemorrhage

D ☐ In acute bleeding, barium contrast studies should be performed at the earliest opportunity

E ☐ Radionuclide sulphur–colloid scans can pick up bleeding rates as slow as 0.5 ml/minute

15 Haemorrhoids

Which of the following statements are true?

A ☐ It has clearly been shown that an increase in fibre intake has been associated with a fall in prevalence of haemorrhoids

B ☐ Haemorrhoids are associated with high resting anal pressure

C ☐ Randomized studies have shown no long-term advantage from sclerotherapy over bulk laxatives

D ☐ Diathermy haemorrhoidectomy obviates the need for a 'pedicle tie'

E ☐ The re-admission rate after day-case haemorrhoidectomy is currently over 10%

13 Faecal Incontinence

A True

B At rest the internal smooth muscle sphincter contributes 80% of the resting tone, but when continence is threatened due to increased intrarectal pressure, for example during coughing, the spinal reflexes elicit external sphincter contraction.

C True

D True

E After injury, direct repair of the sphincter is successful in about 80–90%. However, defects greater than 30% of the anal sphincter are less successfully treated by direct repair, and other techniques such a gracilis muscle transposition may be used.

14 Colonic Haemorrhage

A Of those patients admitted to hospital for gastrointestinal haemorrhage in the UK, 80% have a proximal cause, 5% have obscure origins such as from the small bowel or angiodysplasia, while 15% have a colonic cause.

B Diverticula are more common on the left side of the colon, but acute bleeding is seen more often on the right side of the colon and occurs in up to 70% of patients in some series. Bleeding from diverticula stops spontaneously in 80–90% of patients but re-bleeding occurs in about 25%.

C True

D In acute bleeding, barium contrast studies should be discouraged, because they preclude the use of the more profitable investigation of angiography.

E True

15 Haemorrhoids

A Despite widely held beliefs, fibre intake and the prevalence of haemorrhoids are not associated, and an increase in fibre intake has not been shown to be associated with a fall in the prevalence of haemorrhoids.

B True

C True

D True

E Day-case haemorrhoidectomy has been shown to be successful with a re-admission rate of less than 5%.

MCQs

16 Anorectal Sepsis, Abscess and Fistula

Which of the following statements are true?

A ☐ Men have more intramuscular anal glands than women

B ☐ Over 60% of acute abscesses lead to an anal fistula

C ☐ Draining a supralevator abscess directly into the rectum commonly results in an extrasphincteric fistula

D ☐ Endo-anal ultrasound scanning is now more accurate than MRI in assessing fistula tracts

E ☐ A cutting seton takes up to 20 weeks of regular tightening to cut through enough of the sphincter to allow fistulotomy

17 Laparotomy, Wound Closure and Repair of Incisional Hernias

Which of the following statements are true?

A ☐ Burst abdomen causes a mortality of 15–30%

B ☐ Following a burst abdomen, the first move is to pass a nasogastric tube to prevent vomiting

C ☐ Incisional hernias are asymptomatic in up to 75% of patients

D ☐ Induction of a pneumoperitoneum over 2–3 weeks before repairing a large incisional hernia offers significant benefit

E ☐ After mesh repair of an incisional hernia, there are significant problems if any re-laparotomy is required in the future

18 Anal Fissure

Which of the following statements are true?

A ☐ Myogenic activity of the internal sphincter is characterized by ultra slow wave pressure fluctuations

B ☐ Blood flow to the anoderm at the fissure site is significantly increased compared with normal controls

C ☐ Randomized trials have demonstrated the benefit of regular use of an anal dilator

D ☐ Botulinum toxin injection provides an adequate chemical sphincterotomy

E ☐ After operative anal dilatation, up to 14% of patients develop faecal incontinence

16 Anorectal Sepsis, Abscess and Fistula

A True

B Anal fistulas arise from intramuscular anal gland abscesses but only 15–30% of acute abscesses lead to an anal fistula.

C Draining a supralevator abscess through the levator muscle may result in an extrasphincteric fistula, and so draining it via the rectum is preferable when possible.

D Endo-anal ultrasound is excellent for defining sphincter integrity but it is less accurate than MRI in assessing fistula tracts and is especially poor in the ischiorectal fossa.

E True

17 Laparotomy, Wound Closure and Repair of Incisional Hernia

A True

B Following a burst abdomen, the passage of a nasogastric tube should be avoided in the acute phase, because the associated retching causes the abdominal contents to protrude even further through the wound and may result in the inhalation of vomitus.

C True

D Induction of a pneumoperitoneum over 2–3 weeks before attempted closure of an incisional hernia has been shown to offer no real advantage or benefit.

E After repair of an incisional hernia, one of the advantages of a mesh repair is the ease with which re-operation can be carried out. An incision can be made through the mesh which can then be simply resutured at the end of the procedure.

18 Anal Fissure

A True

B Laser Doppler flowmetry, combined with anorectal manometry, confirms that blood flow to the anoderm at the fissure site is *lower* than in controls.

C Randomized trials have shown that regular use of an anal dilator has been seen to provide no benefit to sufferers of anal fissure, and the pain produced during use causes many patients to abandon this line of treatment.

D True

E True

MCQs

19 Diverticular Disease

Which of the following statements are true?

A ☐ Colonic diverticula are produced by pulsion forces

B ☐ Lower gastrointestinal haemorrhage from diverticular disease seldom occurs without clinical signs of acute diverticulitis

C ☐ An erect chest radiograph reveals free intraperitoneal gas in about 60% of patients with a colonic perforation

D ☐ CT scanning is the investigation of choice in complex diverticular disease

E ☐ Colonoscopy is the procedure of choice during an attack of diverticulitis

20 Inflammatory Bowel Disease

Which of the following statements are true?

A ☐ Smoking protects patients with ulcerative colitis from attacks

B ☐ The anus is involved in up to 45% of patients with Crohn's disease

C ☐ Unlike ulcerative colitis, acute toxic dilatation does not occur in Crohn's colitis

D ☐ During surgery for Crohn's disease all incidentally found asymptomatic lesions should be surgically dealt with to prevent further problems developing

E ☐ In Crohn's disease it is not deemed safe merely to treat fistulas by resection of the affected segment with primary closure of the secondarily affected organ

21 Enterocutaneous Fistulas

Which of the following statements are true?

A ☐ A high-output pancreatic fistula is one in which the output exceeds 200 ml/day

B ☐ In Crohn's disease, type 1 fistulas are those that respond to elemental diets or parenteral nutrition

C ☐ The control of sepsis in patients with intestinal fistulas requires prolonged antibiotic usage

D ☐ In the presence of active infection, only aggressive nutritional support will reverse the catabolic state

E ☐ Provided sepsis has been controlled, 60% of enterocutaneous fistulas will close spontaneously within 1 month

MCQs

19 Diverticular Disease

A True

B Haemorrhage does not generally occur as a feature of acute diverticulitis and, though local inflammation causes the initial vessel damage, lower gastrointestinal haemorrhage associated with diverticular disease usually occurs in the absence of clinical signs of diverticulitis.

C True

D True

E Colonoscopy is usually contraindicated during or soon after an attack of acute diverticulitis.

20 Inflammatory Bowel Disease

A True

B True

C Although acute toxic dilatation is less common in Crohn's disease than in ulcerative colitis, it may still occur and is usually seen in younger patients with a short duration of symptoms.

D During surgery for Crohn's disease all clinically significant fibrostenotic lesions should be dealt with but incidental asymptomatic lesions should be left alone.

E Fistulas may be treated safely by resection of the affected segment of bowel in which the fistula originates, with primary closure of the secondarily affected organ.

21 Enterocutaneous Fistulas

A True

B Type 1 fistulas in Crohn's disease may occasionally close temporarily with elemental diets or parenteral nutrition but renewed fistulation is almost inevitable and these fistulas are best treated by surgical excision.

C Antibiotic therapy may be required for the treatment of any surrounding cellulitis but prolonged use should be avoided because it encourages the development of antibiotic resistance and opportunistic infections.

D In the presence of sepsis, not even aggressive nutritional support will result in a reversal of the catabolic state. All sepsis should be drained.

E True

MCQs

22 Intestinal Obstruction

Which of the following statements are true?

A ☐ The target sign on ultrasound is associated with gallstone ileus

B ☐ CT scan will identify obstruction in up to 95% of patients

C ☐ In intestinal obstruction, potassium losses are revealed more directly by biochemistry than sodium losses

D ☐ In Ogilvie's syndrome of functional colonic obstruction, neostigmine is preferred over colonoscopy under sedation in patients with ischaemic heart disease

E ☐ Radiation-induced strictures may present after a delayed interval of some years

23 Endocrine Tumours of the Pancreas

Which of the following statements are true?

A ☐ Gastrinoma is the single most common functioning endocrine tumour of the pancreas

B ☐ Digital palpation of the pancreas after full mobilization has a sensitivity of 75–95% in locating the tumour

C ☐ After successful resection of an insulinoma, transient hyperglycaemia may take 2–3 weeks to return to normal

D ☐ Surgical resection is a curative procedure in 90% of patients with an insulinoma

E ☐ In MEN-I, gastrinomas are usually benign single lesions

24 Small Bowel Tumours

Which of the following statements are true?

A ☐ Over 75% of benign small bowel tumours present with intestinal obstruction

B ☐ Angiography is now more sensitive at localizing blood loss than radiolabelled red blood cells scans

C ☐ Duodenal carcinoma is the most common cause of death in patients with familial adenomatous polyposis

D ☐ Duodenal gastrinomas account for up to 40% of all gastrinomas

E ☐ At the time of presentation, over 50% of patients with small bowel adenocarcinomas have metastatic spread

22 Intestinal Obstruction

A The target sign on ultrasound scanning is associated with childhood intussusception.

B True

C True

D Ischaemic heart disease is a contraindication to the use of neostigmine.

E True

23 Endocrine Tumours of the Pancreas

A True

B Sensitivity of faecal occult blood testing is low because it fails to detect 20–50% of cancers and up to 80% of polyps.

C True

D Recent randomized trials using carcino-embryonic antigen (CEA) levels for monitoring post-operative recurrence have failed to demonstrate any survival advantage.

E True

24 Small Bowel Tumours

A Unlike malignant lesions, over 50% of benign small bowel tumours are found incidentally at laparotomy or post mortem.

B Angiography localizes haemorrhage when the blood loss is as low as 0.5 ml/minute but red blood cell scans may be positive with blood loss as low as 0.1 ml/minute.

C True

D True

E True

MCQs

25 Anatomy of the Anterior Abdominal Wall

In the abdominal wall:

A ☐ The deep inguinal ring lies 2 cm above the mid-inguinal point

B ☐ The linea semilunaris marks the abrupt change in the arrangement of the posterior rectus sheath and where all three aponeuroses run anterior to the rectus muscle

C ☐ The dermatome of the 7th intercostal nerve is at the level of the epigastrum

D ☐ Scarpa's fascia is very poorly developed in infants

E ☐ The fascia transversalis of the posterior wall of the inguinal canal is reinforced on its anterior surface medially by the conjoint tendon

26 Gastro-oesophageal Reflux Disease

Which of the following statements are true?

A ☐ Medical treatment does not alter the natural history of gastro-oesophageal reflux disease

B ☐ With current management the incidence of Barrett's esophagus is decreasing

C ☐ Patients with gastro-oesophageal reflux disease and oesophageal hypomobility are likely to develop dysphagia after a Nissen fundoplication

D ☐ Normally the pH in the oesophagus is less than 4 for about 2% of the time

E ☐ After treatment with a proton pump inhibitor, up to 20% of patients will have persistent oesophagitis

27 Investigation and Management of Obstructive Jaundice

In the jaundiced patient:

A ☐ Anaerobic organisms are more commonly isolated from patients who have had previous biliary surgery

B ☐ Diffuse liver disease may obscure dilated intrahepatic ducts

C ☐ Failure to cannulate at endoscopic retrograde cholangiopancreatography (ERCP) is most commonly the result of subampullary stenosis

D ☐ After ERCP, severe life-threatening pancreatitis is seen in about 3% of patients

E ☐ With the Mirizzi syndrome, a stone impacted in Hartmann's pouch can cause a cholecystodochal fistula

25 Anatomy of the Anterior Abdominal Wall

A The deep inguinal ring lies 2 cm above the mid-point of the inguinal ligament, rather than above the mid-inguinal point.

B The linea semilunaris is a longitudinal shallow furrow with a gentle lateral convexity extending from the tip of the 9th costal cartilage to the pubic tubercle and denotes the outer margin of the rectus abdominis muscle.

C True

D Scarpa's fascia is in fact very much more prominent in children and infants than in adults.

E True

26 Gastro-oesophageal Reflux Disease

A True

B On the contrary, in spite of all correct therapy, the incidence of Barrett's oesophagus is increasing.

C True

D True

E True

27 Investigation and Management of Obstructive Jaundice

A True

B True

C Failure to cannulate at ERCP is usually the result of the endoscopist not inserting the cannula at the correct angle. Very occasionally, failure is the result of an impacted stone, stenosis or tumour.

D After ERCP, self-limiting pancreatitis occurs in about 3% of patients but severe life-threatening pancreatitis is seen in only about 0.1%.

E True

MCQs

28 The Acute Abdomen

In the acute abdomen:

A ☐ The visceral peritoneum is insensitive to normally painful stimuli

B ☐ The pain fibres in the splanchnic nerves are derived from the parasympathetic nervous system

C ☐ The symptoms of malaise, nausea, vomiting and sweating are often absent in purely somatic pain

D ☐ Analgesia must be witheld until a diagnosis is made or serious pathology will be missed

E ☐ Gross gaseous distension will muffle transmitted heart sounds

29 Management of Peritonitis and Appendicitis

In cases of peritonitis:

A ☐ A raised serum amylase is specific to acute pancreatitis

B ☐ Catarrhal appendicitis seldom progresses to gangrene and perforation

C ☐ Pain on flexion of the hip suggests psoas irritation from a retroperitoneal appendicitis

D ☐ Several studies have shown that rectal examination is a better predictor of appendicitis than abdominal examination

E ☐ Ultrasound scanning for diagnosing appendicitis has a specificity approaching 100%

30 Acute Pancreatitis

In patients with acute pancreatitis:

A ☐ More than 30% may be idiopathic

B ☐ The amalyse:creatine clearance is highly specific

C ☐ Morphine and strong opioids are often required and advantageous as they relax the sphincter of Oddi

D ☐ Surgery for pancreatic necrosis to resect the sequestrum should always be undertaken within the first week

E ☐ Endoscopic pancreaticocystgastrostomy requires a stent to maintain patency

28 The Acute Abdomen

A True

B The splanchnic nerves are derived from the sympathetic system, and include pain fibres that travel with the coeliac, superior and inferior mesenteric arteries.

C True

D There is no evidence that serious pathology is missed if analgesia is used appropriately in the acute abdomen. To withhold analgesia until a diagnosis is made is inappropriate and inhumane.

E Gross gaseous distension actually amplifies the transmitted heart sounds during auscultation of the abdomen.

29 Management of Peritonitis and Appendicitis

A A raised serum amylase is not entirely specific to acute pancreatitis and can be raised with other intra-abdominal pathology.

B True

C The hip may be flexed in patients with psoas irritation from a retroperitoneal appendicitis and there may be more pain on attempting to extend the hip.

D Abdominal signs are better predictors of appendicitis than rectal examination, and the latter may be a distressing and often unhelpful test in children.

C True

30 Acute Pancreatitis

A True

B The amylase:creatinine clearance is a tedious and nonspecific test and is seldom performed or needed.

C Stronger opioids may be required in severe acute pancreatitis but morphine is usually avoided because it *constricts* the sphincter of Oddi, though the clinical relevance of this is uncertain.

D During the first week the sequestrum is attached to the surrounding tissues and to attempt to remove it is lethal, causing significant damage and haemorrhage. In most cases surgery can be delayed for 1–2 weeks when the sequestrum can be debrided gently.

E True

MCQs

31 Chronic Pancreatitis

In patients with chronic pancreatitis:

A ☐ Alcohol accounts for 70–80% of all cases

B ☐ Clinically significant protein and fat deficiency related to malabsorption do not occur until more than 90% of glandular function is lost

C ☐ Thoracoscopic splanchnicectomy now provides the chance of a curative approach to the pain problem

D ☐ Stents placed across strictures in the pancreatic duct often cause further stenosis and a progression of the disease process

E ☐ Accessory sphincterotomy is successful in 70% of patients with pancreas divisum who have intermittent symptoms and an obstructive aetiology

32 Clinical Endocrinology of Gastric Function

Which of the following statements are true?

A ☐ ECL cells increase in number in response to continued gastrin stimulation

B ☐ As the gastric pH rises, antral D cells respond by releasing somatostatin

C ☐ *Helicobacter pylori* antral gastritis increases somatostatin mRNA abundance

D ☐ Infection of the gastric corpus by *H. pylori* is associated with an increased acid output

E ☐ Patients with isolated *H. pylori* antral gastritis are hypogastrinaemic

33 Investigation of Abdominal Masses

When investigating abdominal masses:

A ☐ Ultrasound cannot differentiate between simple cysts with haemorrhage and abscesses

B ☐ Ultrasound scanning can identify as little as 100 ml of ascites

C ☐ The quality of the image in CT scanning is impaired in obese patients

D ☐ CT scanning is the image of choice for diagnosing intra-abdominal lymphadenopathy

E ☐ One of the advantages of MRI is that it is very rapid in the production of images

System Module D

31 Chronic Pancreatitis

A True

B True

C Unfortunately, results show that thoracoscopic splanchnicectomy, though widely advocated, is unlikely to provide a curative approach to the pain problem of chronic pancreatitis.

D True

E True

32 Clinical Endocrinology of Gastric Function

A True

B It is as the gastric pH falls that antral D cells respond by releasing somatostatin, which in turn inhibits gastrin release from G cells.

C *H. pylori* antral gastritis has been shown to be associated with a *decrease* in somatostatin mRNA abundance in the antral mucosa.

D Infection of the acid-producing gastric corpus by *H. pylori* is associated with *reduced* acid output. Initially, this probably results from the direct effects of inflammatory mediators (e.g. cytokines, growth factors) on the parietal cell.

E Usually patients with isolated antral gastritis are hypergastrinaemic with increased gastric acid output and thus are at risk of peptic ulcer disease.

33 Investigation of Abdominal Masses

A Ultrasound can differentiate abscesses from simple cysts with haemorrhage by defining a thick irregular wall.

B True

C CT scanning is not affected by excess fat, in fact it helps separate organs in the abdomen and may even improve the image.

D True

E MRI scanning takes considerable time and an abdominal scan may take 30–60 minutes.

MCQs

34 Inflammatory Bowel Disease

In patients with inflammatory bowel disease:

A ☐ Sudden cessation of frequent loose bowel actions is the first sign of resolution of acute severe toxic colitis

B ☐ CT scanning is useful for diagnosing sealed perforations

C ☐ Bleeding is less conspicuous in Crohn's disease than in ulcerative colitis

D ☐ Cyclosporin A can be given as a foam enema

E ☐ Standard surgical treatment for fissures should be applied to Crohn's fissures

35 Pelvic Inflammatory Disease

Pelvic inflammatory disease:

A ☐ Is decreasing in incidence in developed countries

B ☐ After intrauterine contraceptive device (IUCD) insertion increases in incidence after 3 years

C ☐ Has *Chlamydia trachomatis* as its principal underlying infective agent, being implicated in at least 50% of patients

D ☐ Is caused by *Ureaplasma* and *Mycoplasma* in about 30% of patients

E ☐ When clinically suspected, should be treated immediately with empirical antibiotics rather than waiting until microbiological test results are available

36 Common Abdominal Emergencies

In patients who have sustained an acute perforation:

A ☐ A covered expandable metal stent may be used in those cases of spontaneous perforations of less than 24 hours' duration

B ☐ Abdominal trauma accounts for about 40% of all bowel perforations

C ☐ The caecum, being the weakest part of the colon, is the most common site of perforation

D ☐ Perforation is more common in toxic megacolon caused by Crohn's disease than in that caused by ulcerative colitis

E ☐ A defunctioning proximal stoma does not protect against continuing faecal contamination from a perforated segment of colon

34 Inflammatory Bowel Disease

A Sudden cessation of frequent loose motions is a worrying feature in acute severe toxic colitis and may represent a life-threatening complication such as toxic megacolon and/or perforation.

B True

C True

D True

E Perianal surgery in Crohn's disease should be conservative and standard treatment of fissures for Crohn's fissures should be avoided.

35 Pelvic Inflammatory Disease

A The incidence of pelvic inflammatory disease has increased in developed countries over the last 30 years and now affects about 11% of women of reproductive age at some time.

B The risk of pelvic inflammatory disease is greatest in the first 3 months of IUCD use.

C True

D *Ureaplasma and Mycoplasma* are found in the urinary tract in about 50% of healthy sexually active women but their role in the aetiology of pelvic inflammatory disease is uncertain.

E True

36 Common Abdominal Emergencies

A A covered expandable metal stent can be used for instrumental perforations of malignant disease, but spontaneous perforations of less than 24 hours should be treated surgically.

B True

C The caecum, although the weakest part of the colon, accounts for only about 15% of colonic perforations, usually secondary to a distal obstructing carcinoma. Diverticular disease and carcinoma account for about 80% of all colonic perforations, which is why 70% of perforations occur in the sigmoid colon.

D Perforation may complicate a toxic megacolon secondary to ulcerative colitis but is uncommon in toxic megacolon resulting from Crohn's disease.

E True

EMQs

37 Theme: Bile Duct Stones

A Endoscopic sphincterotomy and basket or balloon stone removal

B Laparoscopic transcystic duct exploration

C Choledochoduodenostomy

D Finish the procedure and rely on postoperative endoscopic retrograde cholangiopancreatography (ERCP) and sphincterotomy

E Postoperative percutaneous stone removal using the Burhenne technique

F Conversion to an open procedure with exploration of the bile duct

G Transduodenal sphincteroplasty

H Extracorporeal shock wave lithotripsy

I Endoscopic placement of an endoprosthesis

For each of the clinical scenarios described below (1–3), select the most suitable line of management from the options listed above (A–I). Each option may be used once, more than once or not at all.

1 ☐ A patient, who has previously undergone a Pólya's gastrectomy, is found to have a retained stone after cholecystectomy.

2 ☐ A very experienced laparoscopic surgeon finds a common duct stone on an operative cholangiogram performed during a laparoscopic cholecystectomy.

3 ☐ An elderly, unfit, jaundiced male is found to have several very large stones impacted within the common bile duct.

38 Theme: Gastro-oesophageal Reflux Disease

A H_2 antagonists   E Laparoscopic Nissen fundoplication

B Proton pump inhibitors   F Belsey mark IV procedure

C Oesophageal dilatation   G Collis gastroplasty

D Photodynamic therapy   H Oesophagectomy

For each of the clinical scenarios described below (1–3), select the single most appropriate treatment from the options listed above (A–H). Each option may be used once, more than once or not at all.

1 ☐ A 65-year-old man with confirmed high-grade dysplasia in a Barrett's oesophagus on two separate endoscopic biopsies

2 ☐ A 50-year-old woman with proven gastro-oesophageal reflux disease and significant bile reflux in addition to the acid

3 ☐ A 61-year-old woman with gastro-oesophageal reflux disease, poor motility and oesophageal shortening manifested by a non-reducible hiatus hernia

EMQs

System Module D

39 Theme: Perianal Conditions

A Anal fissure
B Anal fistula
C Perianal haematoma
D Ischiorectal fossa abscess

E Pilonidal sinus
F Perianal abscess
G Prolapsed thrombosed haemorrhoid
H Proctalgia fugax

For each of the clinical scenarios described below (1–4), select the most likely diagnosis from the options listed above (A–H). Each option may be used once, more than once or not at all.

1 ☐ A 25-year-old man complains of severe anorectal pain that is intermittent and spasmodic, often occurring after intercourse.

2 ☐ A 19-year-old man complains of pain, bleeding and discharge from a mid-line opening 6 cm posterior to the anal verge with a palpable tract leading laterally and cephalad.

3 ☐ A 25-year-old woman complains of an acute painful subcutaneous swelling resembling a blackcurrant which is sited just at the anal verge. She thinks it followed an episode of straining at stool.

4 ☐ A 10-year-old child complains of severe pain after defaecation and a little bright red rectal bleeding is noted on the toilet paper.

40 Theme: Investigation of the Biliary Tree

A Ultrasonography
B Radionuclide scan
C Arteriography
D CT
E Percutaneous transhepatic cholangiography
F MRI
G Endoscopic retrograde cholangiopancreatography (ERCP)
H Barium studies

For each of the clinical scenarios described below (1–4), select the most likely next investigation from the options listed above (A–H). Each option may be used once, more than once or not at all.

1 ☐ A 70-year-old man who underwent Pólya gastrectomy for carcinoma of the stomach develops obstructive jaundice. Ultrasonography and CT show dilated intrahepatic ducts and a mass at the porta hepatis.

2 ☐ An 82-year-old woman presents with cholangitis and is already known to have gallstones.

3 ☐ A 42-year-old woman presents with severe acute abdominal pain and vomiting. The pain radiates through to the back and she is found to have an elevated serum amylase.

4 ☐ A 66-year-old man presents with jaundice, pruritus, dark urine and pale stools. He complains of upper abdominal discomfort and nausea.

Answers: 39 1H, 2E, 3C, 4A; **40** 1E, 2G, 3A, 4A

EMQs

41 Theme: Surgery for Diverticular Disease

A Sigmoid colectomy with primary anastomosis

B Sigmoid colectomy with primary anastomosis and covering loop stoma

C Proximal defunctioning stoma

D Percutaneous drainage of abscess under CT or ultrasound guidance

E Sigmoid colectomy with end colostomy and exteriorization of distal stump as mucous fistula (Devine's procedure)

F Sigmoid colectomy with end colostomy and oversewing of rectal stump (Hartmann's procedure)

For each of the clinical scenarios described below (1–4), select the most appropriate initial operative procedure from the options listed above (A–F). Each option may be used once, more than once or not at all.

1 ☐ A 75-year-old obese woman was admitted as an emergency with faecal peritonitis and was found at laparotomy to have a free perforation of diverticular disease just above the rectosigmoid junction.

2 ☐ An 82-year-old woman, who had suffered from a stroke recently, had become constipated and then developed pain and tenderness in the left iliac fossa. She was admitted as an emergency from her nursing home with a swinging fever, left iliac fossa tenderness, and a palpable mass but the rest of the abdomen was soft with normal bowel sounds.

3 ☐ A 75-year-old man had suffered several attacks of diverticulitis and now was having increasing trouble with his bowels with constipation, distension at times and the passage of mucus. Barium enema revealed a stricture of the sigmoid colon and severe diverticular change.

4 ☐ An 80-year-old woman, who had been admitted twice in the past with profuse lower gastrointestinal haemorrhage, suffered a further bleed. Visceral angiography confirmed that the bleeding was coming from the lower sigmoid colon in an area known to be affected by marked diverticular disease. The patient was otherwise well and had no other symptoms or physical signs.

System Module D

42 Theme: Intestinal Obstruction

A Adhesiolysis

B Extended right hemicolectomy

C Three-stage approach with defunctioning colostomy, colon resection and closure of colostomy

D Hartmann's procedure

E Subtotal colectomy and ileorectal anastomosis

F Colonoscopic decompression

G Intestinal stenting

H Noble's intestinal plication

For each of the clinical scenarios described below (1–4), select the most suitable therapeutic procedure from the options listed above (A–H). Each option may be used once, more than once or not at all.

1 ☐ A 27-year-old woman with central colicky abdominal pain and dilated loops of bowel with valvulae conniventes. She had suffered from a perforated appendix 6 years previously.

2 ☐ A 76-year-old man with an obstructing neoplastic lesion in the distal transverse colon

3 ☐ An 85-year-old woman who developed gross abdominal distension with little abdominal pain following the pinning of a fractured neck of femur

4 ☐ A 92-year-old man with congestive cardiac failure, bronchopneumonia and on corticosteroids is found to have an obstructing carcinoma of the sigmoid colon.

43 Theme: Complications of Groin Hernias

A Gilmore's groin

B Enthesopathy

C *Reductio en masse*

D Maydl's hernia

E Afferent loop obstruction

F Richter's hernia

G Sliding hernia

H Littré's hernia

For each of the clinical scenarios listed below (1–3), select the single most likely diagnosis from the options listed above (A–H). Each option may be used only once, more than once or not at all.

1 ☐ After taxis, ischaemic bowel can be returned to the abdomen with disastrous consequences.

2 ☐ One wall of the hernial sac is formed by a viscus such as the caecum, which forms part of the hernia but lies ouside the cavity of the sac.

3 ☐ A 'W' shaped loop of small bowel lies within the sac and the intervening loop can become strangulated because of ischaemic pressure at the neck of the sac.

Answers: 42 1A, 2B, 3F, 4G; **43** 1C, 2G, 3D

EMQs

44 Theme: Gastrointestinal Haemorrhage

A Oesophageal varices   E Angiodysplasia
B Mallory–Weiss tear   F Ischaemic colitis
C Gastric neoplasm   G Diverticular disease
D Meckel's diverticulum   H Fissure *in ano*

For each of the clinical vignettes listed below (1–4), select the single most likely diagnosis from the options listed above (A–H). Each option may be used once, more than once or not at all.

1 ☐ An episode of moderate and self-limiting bleeding occurring in a 35-year-old man who was admitted retching and vomiting blood after an alcoholic binge

2 ☐ A 70-year-old woman with angina and no previous history of bowel disease is admitted with acute left-sided abdominal pain and copious bloody diarrhoea

3 ☐ A 64-year-old male publican with a large volume haematemesis

4 ☐ A 69-year-old woman presents with anaemia, weight loss and anorexia. She has no overt bleeding

45 Theme: Common Anal and Perianal Disorders

A Haemorrhoids   F Anal fistula
B Anal fissure   G Hidradenitis suppurativa
C Anal canal carcinoma   H Proctalgia fugax
D Inflammatory bowel disease   I Coccydynia
E Solitary rectal ulcer

For each of the clinical scenarios listed below (1–3), select the single most likely diagnosis from the options listed above (A–I). Each option may be used once, more than once or not at all.

1 ☐ A 35-year-old man presents with severe rectal pain that comes in waves. The onset is sudden and it is associated with a sense of dizziness. It is occasionally precipitated by sexual intercourse

2 ☐ A 50-year-old man presents with bright red rectal bleeding that is painless. He first noticed blood on the toilet paper but subsequently found it in the pan. There was no change in his bowel habit and he was otherwise well. The general practitioner reported that rectal examination was normal

3 ☐ A 24-year-old woman who had given birth to a fit, healthy child 3 months previously presents with intensely painful defecation with bright red rectal bleeding. She had tended towards constipation during and since her pregnancy and complained that there was a small swelling at the anal margin that was associated with itching.

EMQs

System Module D

46 Theme: Intestinal Obstruction

A Simple small bowel obstruction

B Strangulating small bowel obstruction

C Sigmoid volvulus

D Gallstone ileus

E Pseudo-obstruction

F Diverticular disease

G Malignant large bowel obstruction

H Caecal volvulus

For each of the case histories listed below (1–4), select the single most likely condition from the options listed above (A–H). Each option may be used once, more than once or not at all.

1 ☐ A 73-year-old man presents with a 3-month history of change in bowel habit, loss of weight and lethargy. Over the past 2 days he has had absolute constipation, increasing distension and lower abdominal pain. The rectum is empty and radiographs show gas-filled loops of bowel demonstrating haustra.

2 ☐ An 86-year-old woman presents with central colicky abdominal pain and vomiting. She has a tachycardia and is febrile, and complains that the pain has become constant over the past few hours. She is found to have a tender lump in her left groin.

3 ☐ A 77-year-old woman presents with marked vomiting and colicky abdominal pain. She is modestly distended and radiographs show distended loops of bowel with valvulae conniventes, as well as pneumobilia.

4 ☐ A demented 82-year-old man is admitted from a nursing home with gross abdominal distension. History is not obtainable from the patient but he does appear in some discomfort. The abdomen is grossly distended but relatively non-tender. Radiographs reveal gross dilatation of the large bowel with a 'coffee-bean' shaped loop arising out of the left lower quadrant.

MCQs

1 Urethral Injuries

Which of the following statements are true?

A ☐ The incidence of anterior urethral injuries is only one-third that of posterior urethral injuries

B ☐ A posterior rupture of the urethra associated with pelvic injuries is incomplete in 65% of patients

C ☐ There must be rupture of Colles' fascia before the characteristic 'butterfly' pattern of bruising in the perineum is seen with anterior urethral injuries

D ☐ Urethrography and cystography are performed at about 3 months if delayed or late repair of a urethral injury is being considered

E ☐ Immediate repair of posterior urethral injuries is associated with a lower incidence of strictures and incontinence

2 Bladder Injuries

Which of the following statements are true?

A ☐ In children up to 6 years of age, the bladder is located intra-abdominally

B ☐ Extravasation of urine is suggested by a rise in blood creatinine in the absence of a commensurate rise in urea

C ☐ CT scanning is an excellent investigation for the accurate diagnosis of bladder rupture

D ☐ Most intraperitoneal ruptures of the bladder can be treated conservatively by adequate bladder drainage

E ☐ The three-swab methylene blue test can distinguish a ureteric from a vesical fistula into the vagina

3 Trauma to the Upper Urinary Tract

Which of the following statements are true?

A ☐ Dipstick detection of microscopic haematuria has a 5% false-positive rate

B ☐ Complete failure of contrast excretion on intravenous urogram (IVU) is an absolute indication for selective arteriography

C ☐ After trauma, the appearance of a cortical rim of contrast on IVU is a reassuring sign because it excludes renal artery occlusion

D ☐ Gerota's fascia should always be opened in suspected perinephric bleeding to prevent pressure damage on the renal cortical parenchyma

E ☐ Surgical intervention for isolated renal artery intimal damage is associated with excellent long-term results

MCQs

1 Urethral Injuries

A True

B The posterior urethra has a close relationship with the bony pelvis and is often associated with serious injury to the pelvis and lower abdomen. In 65% of patients the posterior urethra rupture is *complete.*

C In rupture of the anterior urethra, extension of the haematoma beyond the shaft of the penis depends on rupture of Buck's fascia, in which case the intact Colles' fascia acts as the limiting tissue. This results in the characteristic butterfly pattern of bruising in the perineum.

D True

E Immediate repair of posterior urethral injuries is usually associated with a *higher* incidence of strictures, incontinence and impotence.

2 Bladder Injuries

A True

B A rise in blood urea in the absence of a commensurate rise in creatinine is suggestive of extravasation of urine.

C A CT scan is an excellent investigation tool in renal injuries but is relatively insensitive for the diagnosis of bladder rupture.

D Intraperitoneal rupture of the bladder generally requires surgical exploration with watertight suture of the breached area. Extraperitoneal ruptures are often treated successfully by conservative means using adequate bladder drainage.

E True

3 Trauma to the Upper Urinary Tract

A True

B True

C Intravenous urography with CT is more sensitive than traditional urography and therefore the appearance of a cortical rim of contrast does not exclude major renal arterial occlusion because this comes from collateral capsular vessels.

D The kidney is surrounded by a fascial envelope called Gerota's fascia and this may protect the patient from moderate renal haemorrhage by means of a tamponade effect. If this fascia is opened in suspected renal injury this protective tamponade is lost, uncontrollable haemorrhage can occur and may lead to nephrectomy.

E The reported results of surgical intervention for renal arterial intimal damage are disappointing, with most patients developing renal atrophy and secondary renal hypertension.

MCQs

4 Scrotal Trauma

Which of the following statements are true?

A ☐ The cremaster muscle pulls the testis into the inguinal region in response to danger

B ☐ A haematocele is characterized by a firm mass that fails to transilluminate

C ☐ Testicular tumours present with a history of trauma in about 20% of patients

D ☐ Fournier's gangrene is usually associated with a history of significant scrotal trauma

E ☐ Spermatogenesis has been found to be impaired in patients who have undergone scrotal reconstruction after scrotal skin loss

5 Symptomatic Benign Prostatic Hyperplasia

Which of the following statements are true?

A ☐ For uroflowmetry to record reliable flow rates, the passage of a minimum of 50 ml is required

B ☐ Post-micturition residual volumes are obtained easily using transabdominal ultrasonography

C ☐ Finasteride has been shown to produce a reduction in prostate volume of up to 20–30%

D ☐ Use of epithelializing endoprostheses is confined to the elderly and infirm patient with voiding difficulties

E ☐ The results of retropubic prostatectomy are better than transurethral prostatectomy in terms of relief of obstruction

6 Adult Urinary Incontinence

Which of the following statements are true?

A ☐ In women, the bladder neck mechanism is better developed than in men

B ☐ A 10% incidence of incontinence is reported after radical prostatectomy

C ☐ In women, the proximal third of the urethra and the bladder base lie outside the intra-abdominal pressure zone

D ☐ Anterior colporrhaphy is the most appropriate procedure for correcting urethral hypermobility

E ☐ An artificial sphincter will achieve continence in 95% of patients with post-prostatectomy incontinence

System Module E

4 Scrotal Trauma

A True

B True

C True

D Fournier's gangrene of the scrotum is usually unaccompanied by a history of trauma, though occasionally an earlier minor laceration may be reported.

E True

5 Symptomatic Benign Prostatic Hyperplasia

A For reliable flow rates from uroflowmetry a passage of at least 150 ml is recommended.

B True

C True

D True

E True

6 Adult Urinary Incontinence

A In women the bladder neck mechanism is poorly developed and continence depends on a structure analogous to the distal sphincter mechanism in men.

B True

C Women rely on the intra-abdominal position of the proximal third of the urethra and the bladder base so that a rise in intra-abdominal pressure (such as coughing) acting on the bladder is counteracted by a similar pressure on the proximal urethra.

D Anterior colporrhaphy corrects prolapse but has poor long-term results and is inappropriate for correcting urethral hypermobility.

E True

MCQs

7 Urinary Tract Infection

In patients with urinary tract infection:

A ☐ The incidence increases with the presence of sickle cell trait

B ☐ Acute cystitis is adequately treated by a 3-day regimen of antibiotics

C ☐ The strains of *Escherichia coli* that cause acute pyelonephritis are identical to those that cause chronic pyelonephritis and scarring

D ☐ An intravenous urogram is the best investigation for diagnosing chronic pyelonephritis

E ☐ Co-trimoxazole is not recommended in pregnancy

8 Urinary Tract Trauma

In cases of trauma:

A ☐ Microscopic haematuria alone does not require further emergency investigation

B ☐ Avulsion of the renal pedicle is grade III according to the American Association for the Surgery of Trauma (AAST)

C ☐ Bladder injuries are intraperitoneal in 70% of cases

D ☐ After anterior urethral injury a 'butterfly' perineal and scrotal haematoma indicates an intact Buck's fascia

E ☐ Immediate end-to-end repair of urethral injuries results in less morbidity from urethral strictures later

9 Haematuria and Urological Investigations

In investigating the urinary tract:

A ☐ Malignancy is found in up to 28% of patients with microscopic haematuria

B ☐ A urine sample for cytological examination should be an early-morning collection

C ☐ The contrast medium for an intravenous urogram produces unpleasant side-effects in 15% of patients

D ☐ Transrectal ultrasound has a very high sensitivity for diagnosing prostatic carcinoma

E ☐ A urinary flow meter is invaluable for distinguishing bladder outflow obstruction and detrusor failure

7 Urinary Tract Infection

A True

B True

C The strains of *E. coli* that cause acute pyelonephritis are markedly different from those causing chronic pyelonephritis and renal scarring, indicating different strains with different expressions of virulence.

D True

E True

8 Urinary Tract Trauma

A True

B Avulsion of the renal pedicle is actually grade V on the AAST classification.

C Of all bladder injuries, 70% are extraperitoneal and 95% of these are associated with pelvic fractures.

D In cases of anterior urethral rupture, an intact Buck's fascia will result in a 'sleeve' haematoma of the penis. If Buck's fascia is torn but Colles' fascia is intact, the classical 'butterfly' haematoma can be expected.

E True

9 Haematuria and Urological Investigations

A Malignancy is found in only 5% of patients with microscopic haematuria, but in up to 28% of patients with macroscopic haematuria.

B A urine sample for cytological examination must be freshly passed and not an early-morning collection.

C True

D Transrectal ultrasound is unreliable for the detection of prostatic carcinoma because the classical hypoechoic appearance is seen in only 60% of patients. If carcinoma is suspected, therefore, ultrasound-guided biopsies should be taken from about six sites.

E Urinary flow meter measurements merely record flow in ml/second and thus, although low flow occurs with outflow tract problems such as prostatic hyperplasia, it can also occur with detrusor muscle failure.

MCQs

10 Prostatic Carcinoma

Prostatic carcinoma:

A ☐ In England and Wales is the second most common malignancy in men

B ☐ Contains cells that undergo apoptosis with androgen administration

C ☐ Is understaged by 40% when a combination of digital examination and transurethral ultrasonography is used

D ☐ When treated surgically carries a mortality of over 5% for radical prostatectomy

E ☐ Has prostate specific antigen (PSA) level as an important prognostic indicator

11 Renal Tumours

In patients with renal tumours:

A ☐ Oncocytomas are hamartomas consisting of smooth muscle, blood vessels and fat

B ☐ Angiomyolipomas secrete renin which causes primary hyperaldosteronism

C ☐ All adenomas are now considered to be malignant or premalignant

D ☐ Transitional cell carcinomas of the pelvis comprise 6% of renal malignancies

E ☐ There is a 90% cure rate for Wilm's tumours that are limited to the kidney

12 Bladder Cancer

In patients with bladder cancer:

A ☐ There is a higher 5-year survival rate in men than women

B ☐ There is a fourfold increase after radiotherapy to the uterine cervix

C ☐ Even the best imaging is associated with an over-staging by 10%

D ☐ Up to 50% of cases of carcinoma *in situ* are eventually associated with papillary or nodular tumours

E ☐ Ultrasonography is regarded as the imaging modality of choice for haematuria

10 Prostatic Carcinoma

A True

B Prostatic carcinoma cells are sensitive to androgens and undergo apoptosis following androgen ablation.

C True

D Mortality for radical prostatectomy is low and currently is < 1%.

E True

11 Renal Tumours

A Oncocytomas are not hamartomas but well-differentiated tumours arising from the proximal convoluted tubule. However, angiomyolipomas are hamartomas and consist of smooth muscle, blood vessels and fat.

B Angiomyolipomas do not secrete renin or cause hyperaldosteronism, but juxtaglomerular tumours do. These arise from the renal cortex.

C True

D True

E True

12 Bladder Cancer

A True

B True

C True

D True

E True

MCQs

13 Immunosuppressive Agents and Xenotransplantation

Which of the following statements are true?

A ☐ Acute rejection is caused by preformed antibodies in the recipient against donor HLA or ABO antigens

B ☐ Cyclosporin is of particular value in reversing established acute rejection

C ☐ Azathioprine is a prodrug that is converted into 6-mercaptopurine

D ☐ The baboon is a more likely source of xenografts than the pig

E ☐ Xenozoonosis is a greater risk from pigs than from baboons

14 Renal Transplantation

Which of the following statements are true?

A ☐ A minimum 2-year tumour-free interval should have elapsed before a cancer patient receives a transplant

B ☐ The term 'acute rejection' is applied only when there is a deterioration in graft function

C ☐ The upper age limit for donor suitability is now up to 60 years

D ☐ 5-year graft survival for an unrelated donor is about 80–85%

E ☐ Only about 30% of cadaveric kidneys function immediately after transplantation

15 Pancreas Transplantation

Which of the following statements are true?

A ☐ Pancreatic transplantation normalizes glycosylated haemoglobin in insulin dependent diabetic patients

B ☐ A creatinine clearance of > 70 ml/minute is required for pancreatic transplantation

C ☐ In patients with bladder-drained pancreatic transplants, a significant rise in urinary amylase over two successive readings indicates that anti-rejection therapy should be started

D ☐ About 80% of pancreas transplants have been performed with a simultaneous kidney transplant

E ☐ In spite of improving glucose control, pancreatic transplantation does not improve motor or sensory nerve function

129

MCQs

13 Immunosuppressive Agents and Xenotransplantation

A Acute rejection is a predominantly cellular process while hyperacute rejection is caused by preformed antibodies in the recipient against donor HLA or ABO antigens.

B Cyclosporin and tacrolimus are the most important components of the current maintenance immunosuppression regimens but they are unable to reverse established acute rejection.

C True

D Although, from an immunological perspective, it would appear that one of the non-human primates such as the baboon would be the ideal donor of organs for humans, it is more likely that the pig will be the best source of xenografts.

E Xenozoonosis (a disease process of introducing microorganisms with the transplanted organ from donor animal to human) is a much greater risk from non-human primates than from pigs, though the presence of endogenous retroviruses in pigs is also causing some concern.

14 Renal Transplantation

A True

B True

C The criteria for donor suitability are slowly being relaxed and the upper age limit is now 70–80 years.

D True

E Virtually all live donor kidneys and about 60–80% of cadaveric kidneys function immediately after transplantation.

15 Pancreas Transplantation

A True

B The creatinine clearance is used to select patients for simultaneous pancreas and kidney transplantation. Patients with a creatinine clearance < 40 ml/minute tend to receive simultaneous pancreas/kidney transplants, those with a clearance > 70 ml/minute receive pancreas alone, while those with a clearance 40–70 ml/minute may be offered a pre-emptive kidney transplant.

C In those patients with bladder-drained pancreatic transplants, a *fall* in urinary amylase of > 50% over two successive readings is an indication that anti-rejection therapy should be started and a biopsy taken.

D True

E Recent studies have reported improved motor and sensory nerve function, as assessed by nerve conduction velocity, after kidney and pancreas transplants compared to kidney transplants alone.

MCQs

16 Principles of Transplantation

With regard to immunosuppression for transplantation:

A ☐ Induction and maintenance of donor-specific tolerance is now highly effective in humans

B ☐ Tacrolimus tends to be superior to cyclosporin in liver transplantation

C ☐ Anti-T cell agents result in a higher incidence of herpesvirus reactivation

D ☐ Injection of donor cells directly into the thymus is potentiated in adults with an involuted thymus

E ☐ The presence of donor-reactive IgG alloantibodies in the recipient serum is regarded as a contraindication to transplantation

17 Brain Stem Death

In assessing brain stem death:

A ☐ The final timing of death is the time of cessation of the heart beat

B ☐ Testing should take place when the core temperature is low, because this puts less demand on the essential body functions

C ☐ The $Paco_2$ rises rapidly after brain stem death

D ☐ In the UK there is no prescribed time interval between the two required sets of tests for brain stem death

E ☐ The absence of activity on the EEG does not preclude neurological recovery after cerebral ischaemia

18 Renal Transplantation

In renal transplantation:

A ☐ A patient may be accepted for transplantation 2 years after a $T_1N_0M_0$ carcinoma of the breast

B ☐ Patients are deemed unsuitable for transplantation if they have suffered from tuberculosis

C ☐ The outcome of using infant donor kidneys is improved significantly if transplanted into infant recipients

D ☐ Analysis of the effluent from pulsatile perfusion may help identify non-viable kidneys

E ☐ The left kidney of a donor is usually placed in the recipient's left iliac fossa

16 Principles of Transplantation

A Although induction and maintenance of donor-specific tolerance is possible in rodents, it has proved impossible to reproduce in man.

B True

C True

D The injection of donor cells directly into the thymus has been successful in rats, but it is uncertain whether this would be successful in adult humans in whom the thymus has involuted.

E True

17 Brain Stem Death

A In the UK the timing of death is now identified as the time of confirmation of brain stem death and not necessarily the time of cessation of the heart beat.

B Testing for brain stem death should be undertaken with a core temperature above 35°C because a low body temperature can induce deep coma.

C The metabolic rate after brain stem death is low and therefore it takes some time for the Pa_{CO_2} to rise to the required level for testing, which is usually greater than 5.0 kPa.

D True

E True

18 Renal Transplantation

A The risk of recurrence of malignancy in a recipient is usually considered acceptable 2 years after $T_1N_0M_0$ renal cancer but after 5 years for a $T_1N_0M_0$ breast cancer.

B Patients with tuberculosis should complete a year of effective drug treatment and then can be considered for transplantation.

C The poor outcome from infant kidneys is compounded further when transplanted into infant recipients.

D True

E The left kidney of a donor is usually transplanted into the recipient's right iliac fossa, and a right kidney into the left so that the ureter lies uppermost.

MCQs

19 **Liver and Intrathoracic Transplantation**

In the current status of transplantation:

A ☐ A liver graft may be kept at a temperature of 40°C for up to 20 hours of 'cold ischaemia time'

B ☐ Hepatic artery thrombosis of a liver graft in the first week invariably requires retransplantation

C ☐ Transplantation for hepatocellular carcinoma of less than 4 cm diameter is seldom complicated by recurrence

D ☐ The lung is more tolerant of ischaemia than the heart

E ☐ The use of heart/lung transplantation has become less common over the last 15 years

20 **Small Bowel Transplantation**

Which of the following statements are true?

A ☐ Adaptation of the remaining gut in 'short-gut syndrome' is complete after 6 months

B ☐ A patient may survive on enteral feeding with 15 cm of small intestine if the colon and ileocaecal valve is intact

C ☐ Bowel transplantation is contraindicated in TPN-induced cholestasis

D ☐ Currently, about 50% of patients with small bowel transplants require a composite liver/bowel graft

E ☐ After transplantation, the grafted bowel undergoes a transient period of hyperperistalsis

21 **Management of the Multiple Organ Donor**

Which of the following statements are true?

A ☐ CNS malignancy is a contraindication to organ donation

B ☐ After brain stem death there is an increase in circulating T3

C ☐ Cortisol levels are low after brain stem death

D ☐ Diabetes insipidus occurs in about 65% of donors

E ☐ A high positive end-expiratory (PEEP) level should be avoided during respiratory support of the donor

System Module E

MCQs

19 Liver and Intrathoracic Transplantation

A True

B True

C True

D The lung is actually less tolerant of ischaemia than the heart

E True

20 Small Bowel Transplantation

A Adaptation of bowel in the short-gut syndrome is most marked during the first 6 months, but the process may continue for 2–3 years.

B A patient may survive on enteral feeding with 100 cm of small bowel and a terminal stoma, with 60 cm if the colon is retained and with as little as 30 cm if the colon is intact and the ileocaecal valve preserved.

C TPN-induced cholestasis is actually an indication for small bowel transplantation, as is failure of TPN or exhaustion of intravenous access sites.

D True

E True

21 Management of the Multiple Organ Donor

A Malignancy is indeed a contraindication to organ donation, except for the CNS.

B After brain stem death there is actually a decrease in T3 and some workers have linked this with the depression of myocardial function.

C True

D True

E True

MCQs

22 Benign Prostatic Hyperplasia

Benign prostatic hyperplasia:

A ☐ Occurs as a result of hyperplasia of periurethral glands in the transitional zone

B ☐ For effective uroflowmetry, a voiding volume of 150 ml is required

C ☐ An increase in residual urine is a sign of bladder decompensation rather than obstruction *per se*

D ☐ Treatment with finasteride causes a 50% reduction in prostate volume, with a corresponding improvement in clinical symptoms

E ☐ After transurethral resection of the prostate (TURP) there is erectile dysfunction in up to 30% of patients

23 Immune Response to Transplantation

For organ transplantation:

A ☐ The 5-year graft survival rate for liver transplants is 50%

B ☐ The supply of donor hearts is so limited that attempting to match HLA is impractical

C ☐ Immediate or hyperacute rejection is mediated largely by T lymphocytes

D ☐ Azathioprine acts by blocking interleukin-2 (IL-2) receptor binding

E ☐ The placenta provides an immunologically privileged site

24 Testicular Tumours

In patients with testicular tumours:

A ☐ The incidence of germ cell tumours has doubled over the last 20 years

B ☐ An elevated lactate dehydrogenase is a prognostic indicator

C ☐ No orchidectomy should be performed without intraoperative frozen-section confirmation of the diagnosis

D ☐ Elevated levels of α-fetoprotein are found in 75% of patients with pure seminoma

E ☐ Orchidectomy and low-dose irradiation to the para-aortic and pelvic nodes will produce a cure rate of about 98% of stage 1 seminomas

22 Benign Prostatic Hyperplasia

A True

B True

C True

D Finasteride blocks the enzyme 5α-reductase and causes a 20–30% reduction in prostatic volume, but there is only a modest improvement in symptoms.

E True

23 Immune Response to Transplantation

A True

B True

C Immediate or hyperacute rejection is mediated by preformed antibody.

D Azathioprine acts by being cytotoxic to any dividing cell, including T and B lymphocytes. Cyclosporin acts by blocking production of interleukin-2, while rapamycin blocks IL-2 receptor binding but is too toxic for human use.

E True

24 Testicular Tumours

A True

B True

C Frozen-section histology is difficult to interpret and may lead to cell dispersal and therefore is seldom used.

D α-fetoprotein levels are not elevated in patients with pure seminoma but are elevated in 75% of patients with teratoma.

E True

EMQs

25 **Theme: Renal Dysfunction**

A Nephrotic syndrome

B Glomerular nephritis

C Acute pyelonephritis

D Interstitial nephritis

E Chronic pyelonephritis

F Reflux nephritis

G Acute tubular necrosis

For each of the clinical scenarios described below (1–3), select the most likely diagnosis from the options listed above (A–G). Each option may be used once, more than once or not at all.

1 ☐ A patient develops an acute allergic reaction after treatment with an antibiotic. The patient is systemically unwell with a rash and eosinophilia and there is acute loss of renal function with blood and protein in the urine.

2 ☐ A patient with normocytic normochromic anaemia is found to be in chronic renal failure. Ultrasound scanning reveals small, asymmetrically scarred kidneys.

3 ☐ A patient presents with marked peripheral oedema and is found to have a serum albumin of < 30 g/litre and a urinary protein of > 3 g/day.

26 **Theme: Brain Stem Death**

A Hypothermia

B 'Doll's eyes' movements

C Oliguria

D Apnoeic coma

E Absent corneal reflex

F Positive Babinski test

G Absence of local spinal reflexes

H A total absence of EEG activity

For each of the definitions described below (1–3), select the most likely term from the options listed above (A–H). Each option may be used once, more than once or not at all.

1 ☐ This feature is a precondition for the diagnosis of brain stem death.

2 ☐ This condition must be excluded before a diagnosis of brain stem death can be made.

3 ☐ This condition is a formal clinical test in the UK for brain stem death.

System Module E

EMQs

27 **Theme: Treatment of Renal Failure**

A Haemodialysis

B Continuous arteriovenous haemofiltration (CAVH)

C Continuous venovenous haemofiltration (CVVH)

D Haemodiafiltration (CVVH-D)

E Continuous ambulatory peritoneal dialysis (CAPD)

F Continuous cycling peritoneal dialysis (CCPD)

For each of the treatment descriptions listed below (1–3), select the single most likely treatment from the options listed above (A–F). Each option may be used once, more than once or not at all.

1 ☐ This treatment works on the basis of convection with blood flowing under pressure down one side of a highly permeable membrane. It produces an ultrafiltrate and clears urea, creatinine and phosphates at similar rates. Venous blood is removed from the circulation by a double-lumen catheter, pumped through the system and returned to the patient.

2 ☐ This method utilizes the body's natural membrane for dialysis. A hypertonic solution containing no urea is allowed to equilibrate with blood and body water. A Tenckhoff catheter may be used for access and can be used for long-term treatment of chronic renal failure but is contraindicated in the presence of fistulas.

3 ☐ This is a continuous method and allows gradual fluid removal with good extracellular fluid volume control and can be used in hypotensive patients. Almost any quantity of fluid can be removed over a 24-hour period. It depends on venous blood being removed from the body, pumped through the filter and then returned to the body. Its use in acute renal failure has coincided with a reduction in mortality.

28 **Theme: HLA Tissue Typing in Solid Organ Transplantation**

A CD8+ T cells

B HLA molecules

C Allo-MHC antigens

D HLA cytotoxic antibodies

E APC (antigen-presenting cells)

For each of the descriptions below (1–2), select the single most likely option from those listed above (A–E). Each option may be used once, more than once or not at all.

1 ☐ Cell-surface glycoprotein derived from the genes of the class I and II regions

2 ☐ Processes and presents exogenous foreign peptides to the CD4+ T cells of the immune system in association with class II molecules

Answers: 27 1C, 2E, 3C; **28** 1B, 2E

138

System Module E

EMQs

29 Theme: Innervation of the Lower Urinary Tract

A Pudendal nerves (S2–S4)

B Sympathetic via the hypogastric nerves (T10–L2)

C Somatic via the genitofemoral nerve

D Parasympathetic via the pelvic nerves (S2–S4)

E Somatic via the lesser splanchnic nerve

F Ilioinguinal nerve (L1)

For each of the actions of the lower urinary tract listed below (1–4), select the single most likely innervation from the options listed above (A–F). Each option may be used once, more than once or not at all.

1 ☐ Detrusor contraction

2 ☐ Contraction of the bladder neck and proximal urethra

3 ☐ Contraction of the pelvic floor (levator ani)

4 ☐ Detrusor relaxation

30 Theme: Renal Tract Stones

A Conservative management

B Percutaneous management

C Extracorporeal shockwave lithotripsy

D Ureteroscopy

E Open ureterolithotomy

F Laparoscopic ureterolithotomy

For each of the clinical vignettes listed below (1–3), select the single most likely form of management from the options listed above (A–F). Each option may be used once, more than once or not at all.

1 ☐ A 60-year-old man with an 8 mm stone impacted in the upper ureter who is suffering with severe pain, high fever and rigors

2 ☐ A 35-year-old man with a 3.5 mm stone in the ureter with no evidence of obstruction

3 ☐ A 63-year-old woman with a stone in the mid-ureter with a distal ureteric stricture